THE SKELETONS WITHIN:

A Charmed Kreation

~~Exhuming Blood, Tears, Bones~~

Anne O'Kayè

EDITOR: Kya Publishing, Canada
COVER & PAGE DESIGNER: Ashley Mae Pancho (Philippines)
EBOOK DESIGNER: Osamu Diamenabdul (Nigeria)
CONTRIBUTIONS: ElevatedWaves Publishing Corp.

PUBLISHER: Averie's Kreations Inc. (Cleveland, Ohio)
ISBN (Paperback): 979-8-9919599-0-2
ISBN (Ebook): 979-8-9919599-1-9

Library of Congress Control Number: 2024923755

This book may be purchased in bulk for educational, business, or sales promotional use via Kreationsserenitybyokaye@gmail.com

For Bianca A. Dempster,
Thank you for your unwavering support, for almost two decades.

With boundless love and appreciation,
O'Kayè

For A'Mir O.A. Smikle,

You are the sweetest, most supportive kid I have ever met,   and I hope that you continue to blossom into the person you want to be. Your constant warmth and companionship are something that I will never be able to repay, but I will always try to. I am eternally grateful for you.

Finally, let no one place limitations on your success, self-worth, dreams, future, aspirations, or individualism. I love you beyond measure, my sweet nephew.

Always and forever,
your one and only Otay

Table of Contents

CHAPTER IX 271

CHAPTER X 304

I will not say don't date poets

Because if their tongue is any indication then bilingual beings include the most artful of speakers.

Yet, I have seen these same tongue twisting maniacs choreograph the destruction of relationships by serving serenades as manipulative Miranda Rights in arrested attraction, fatal breakups, domestic flights, and Valentine pillow talks all night.

See, in English we start relationships by saying, "you're beautiful," but in poetry we say, "I used to wonder why God forbade the worship of stars until I realized it's mystery is nothing compared to the breathtaking essence radiating through you."

In English we'll say, "teach me how to love you," but in poetry we say, "be the cartographer of my heart, map its rerouted direction to your will so we will never depart."

In English we say, "I hate when you are not with me."

But in poetry we say, "I finally figured out why it is a Jack-the-Ripper sort of torture codifying the untangled collision of our hearts when I watch my feet drum these streets without you."

By the time we see the end we think to cough up famous tired lines so in English we say, "it's not you, it's me." But in poetry we say, "sometimes the rain falls to give the sun a break from shining so much and it is never because he wishes to hurt her."

In English we say don't break my heart for I cannot live without you. But in poetry we say, if it is unnatural to separate peanut butter from jelly then I cannot lose oxygen and be expected to breathe, so if we must part then baby tie this flat line to your wrist and let my heart be the mausoleum under which you rest in peace

In English we say, "remember when I convinced myself that what we had was love?" But in poetry we say, "my heart still gaslights my mind into accepting the premise that this trauma bond of ours was a gift from Aphrodite camouflaged to hide its true identity."

In English we say, "I am not opposed to mourning the loss of love, for it is in the heights of grief that we drink of solace."

But in poetry

In poetry we say, "I scream to be set free for there is a wailing that rises just beyond the pit of my lower gut every time I am Able to view the curse of these dried bones Cain threaded through his blood, and all for the sake of a love that didn't think his sacrifice sufficient."

In English I say, "I cannot date someone who speaks in riddles."

But in poetry I say, "I refuse to give shelter to the soul of another who sews their words of lust with golden spindles."

In English I say, "I have hidden the spare parts of myself from cupid." But in poetry I say, "I still hold all my pieces in the urn that once served as the airway of love."

In English I say, "I cannot date a poet."

But in poetry I say, "I too am the architect that built Babel with the words I cannot trust another tongue twister to build a home in."

The one whose name drips of eradicated pain, for I know all too well how the distance between English and poetry leaves a tornado of wreckage no one else wants to lay claim to.

CHAPTER I
Victimology

'Misery won't touch you gentle. It always leaves its
thumbprints on you; sometimes it leaves them for others to
see, sometimes for nobody but you to know of.'

~ Edwidge Danticat, The Farming of Bones[1]

---

1 "It is not the bruises on the body that hurt. It is the wounds of the heart and
the scars on the mind." ~ Aisha Mirza

Just another S.A Poem

After Ebony Stewart's 'How to write a poem about sexual assault'

Ebony Stewart asked how to write a poem about sexual assault, as if hearing about the violation of no-no parts was enough goodwill principle to guilt people into stopping these acts.

Like assault ain't a bitch livid enough to keep walking alongside catcalls. And ever since I learned that these nubbins on my chest were magnets for bad touches, I have been attempting to write a poem that could see me somewhat healed enough to acknowledge that these things happen far too often, though they shouldn't.

I have spent days avoidant of the lust that drives people to take what is not theirs. Have stood and watched victims jump through every hoop to still get blamed. And I have not yet learned how to write about something that I am too ashamed to say I know firsthand,
too ashamed to give a name to, because it's too big a bounty to pay for, too horrid a topic to warn of, and it's still too heavy a heartache to pass as a personal item on airplanes should I want to throw it over my back and travel with it.

So, I have kept my mouth shut should devils fall from my throat to tell me this is not a topic worth attempting. Because the senility in each repressed memory makes this just another old witch tale that the skin remembers.

I want to tell Ebony Stewart that sometimes the hardest thing
to write about is the most common:
the oceans that slap against banks that do not want them;
the desire to slay dragons of crime that refuses to alleviate
itself and has taken root in our streets;
I want to tell Ebony Stewart that tears and screams are
enough poetry to tell the stories that Oxford has no words for.

I want to tell Ebony Stewart that someday we will find a way
to write a poem loud enough and frequent enough for the
voices lost in the roar of trespassers claiming to be victors
of our bodies.

Because to write a poem about sexual assault is to steal the
backbone of victims from the underbelly of those claiming
themselves to be undefeated.
to strike with the thunder from the bolts of Jupiter
to claw out a scream that this reality is not gender defined,
because predators shapeshift too and that is why we always
choose the bear.

So when you want to write a poem about sexual assault,
begin by striping the flames from your throat and then spit
it into the air, Percy Jackson hydrokinesis every attack into
a drowning that will shock Noah.

The sort of flood raging beneath Bartholin's glands and
then, sit back to watch 300 cubits become the Titanic's only
company.

What do you call a secret that irrigates flowers blooming from Lucifer's throat?

Do you call it foreign? Do you call it necrosis?
Do you call it stillbirth or rainbow baby?
Do you figure out how hard it is to unhitch a secret
forged in shame and uncertainty pushing itself up from
your womb?
A secret survived for years settled as a never ending
battalion of haints that scorches the raw streets of hades
That pry open storm clouds to find out how something
so puffy and soft could bring so much rage

What do you call a secret of seven tongues?
How do you name a secret that has lived in the homes of
so many different cultures?
Do you call it diverse?
Do you know how hard it is to protect a secret that
breaks your back and gumbo stir your bones into the
latest banshee curse?
Do you know how to butterfly stitch a truth so hard
it becomes the cessation of a never healing wound in
your gut?
becomes the trailing of the Spurinna's warnings
Do you know how hard it is to rinse a secret from
your throat?
How to croak out a fraction of something that builds a
breaking within
your jawbone?

What's the price of a secret when you can't hold on to it
anymore?
When all the outside can't unravel the bloodlust within
Can't set your bones back in place
Can't wipe your mind clean
Does a secret have the ability to skin you and leave
herself naked and shivering at your doorstep?
Like abandoned babes swaddled in fire stations with the
hope this will become security
Does it become you, or a taunting of relief when it severs
itself from your tongue, no longer ashamed
of what you are?
Does it become less of a burden when it is removed from
its leash or more of a target?
Does it give itself a new name or does it struggle to be
either revenge or healing when it figures that it cannot
be both?

Is it abuse if you push but don't scream

Is it abuse if you wake up all out of fights or f**ks to give
any more? Is it abuse if you've become a poster child for
panic and paralysis?

[2]If you bargain with both the Devil and God, hoping to get
a good deal on death
is it abuse if silence becomes a constant companion, if
speaking makes it more real
if crying makes you weak or vulnerable
if fighting someone off you isn't enough to get them out of
your DNA, out of your head
their voice from your ears
is it abuse if you dig a well for the memories,
if you noose the feel of your skin in sulfuric acid
if you forget what you wanted dead instead of focusing on
what's easier to kill

Is it abuse if you find God reversing your blood back into
you
if you carve an expiration promise on your thighs and
arms so as to never get this hurt again
is it abuse if silence is the only comfort worth the effort
and the claustrophobic walls and bed sheets are the only
ones that know the truth
is it still abuse if he apologized right after
if every time he forces you open he tells you he is only
doing his job as a

...

2 *"The supreme art of war is to subdue the enemy without fighting."* ~ Sun
Tzu, The Art of War

is it abuse if you don't break until years after when poetry
and art and nothing becomes a companion
willing and strong enough to wash the pain away

and do you ever stop giving a f**k what anyone has to say
about you or how long you waited to unstitch your

wired jaw

A girl kills her memories before she can learn to carve

it into sacrifice or gospel
She places it near her heart so it becomes a powerful
wind, enough to build a fire within her
and she uses that fire to light a match under her tongue
heated enough to save the girl who sleeps beside her
the girl whose screams can make a farshee blush

The girl whose tears can melt gold and she never wants
her to live like her or grow like her
holding all emotions to the light like they were protection
for private parts, and she holds her breath for all to hate
her as a family collapses around the shackles of the truth
and the girl shoves her memories before her to become a
ban nigheachain prophet soothing her own destruction.

To live in the body of a survivor is to always be at odds with yourself

Is to frequently transition between purity and pollution
without knowing which one tomorrow brings
Or which one you ultimately assimilate into

To live in the body of a survivor means to drown yourself
in waters that don't always glisten and call it a bath.
Call it recharged electrolytes.

To live in the body of a survivor is to be a watch guard for
a cemetery that consistently coughs up grave robbers and
dust mites and a clone of its own [3]skeletons and calls all that
a treasure chest pirates would be lucky to steal.

To live in the body of a survivor is to unwrap each expression
and tone with delicacy so much so that you are not called
a bitch because of the bitterness oiling itself across the
canvas of your back.

To live in the body of a survivor is to fold your memories
into tiny blisters and call it home-cooked and glorified; call
it anything but salvation or beauty; call it withered love; but
never call it a body that has not survived because to live in
the body of a survivor means to befriend death and borrow
her pink pants on occasion.

Is to befriend depression

3 *"Scars have the strange power to remind us that our past is real."*
~ Cormac McCarthy

Is to adopt self-love and then sabotage and split each down the middle so you can close your eyes and give one as a rose to the things you have survived and keep another as a reminder for the things you must slaughter moving forward.

Humorless rape joke

The joke is told that the difference between a rape victim and a marriage is that with a marriage, you are obligated to keep the screaming woman afterward.
And they think it's funny to coin jeers after the pain of others as if part of their life isn't stripped away too soon.

And if life goes on, then how come,
How come a victim goes to a party and sees herself sprawled across the floor from mouth bullets that were meant to take her dignity to the level of dogs.

A victim confesses her sins of hatred in pews meant to light her way to God, and priests turn their noses up at her, refusing her tickets on the bus of the saints.
A victim becomes another story told of mythological characters to children in revealing clothing and houses a strap-on should she have to f**k her way out of this mess, because they don't believe that her clothes were not an invitation to share her body.

A victim walks into a bar, sits at a table, and drinks one too many over her limit but is still sober enough to say "no" loud enough for all to hear, only no one believes that her "no" really means "no," so they take her to the pleasure fields she refuses to walk.

A victim calls herself No Man's Land and is called queer, called vermin to society is called unconventional, called ruined.

A victim exhales her truth and is called a cross between bitter and ghetto, as if the unsavory acts committed against her were a way to keep her in her place.
And
They say she has not yet learned her lesson.

A victim is raped once and is asked to get over it, but she offends the rulers when she spits the ways of the hood.

A victim is charged when she grabs her sexuality back from the claws of lawmen claiming indecent exposure,
but she never once forgets that she is still a banshee exercising her right to keep the ears of men bleeding, and she finds her justice through her singing.

I used to believe in Santa Claus the way I believed in the sun rising every morning[4]

I used to believe in authors like they were prophets who could make the occupants of gilded cages sing as sweetly as mockingbirds. And I still do, only their prophecies never came through so I started believing in the miracles of Christmas, started believing that Santa Claus only came to the obedient until I realized that my father and Santa shared an MO.

Until I saw them morph into myths

Until they saw me sleeping and awake, because omnipresent Santa Claus sees all when he comes to town, especially when no doors are inside this house.

And I don't remember if that was when I swore off Christmas and every make-belief contraption they called great
Don't know if that was when I laid in wake of the Tooth Fairy should he take more than a tooth
Don't know if that was when I went silent, hoping that I would find coins that wouldn't burn through my hands
That wouldn't itch like cowitch leaves

Don't know if that was when I hated everything joyous

And at fourteen I never wanted Santa Claus to come to town before I got the chance to be armed with
guns or knives or brass knuckles or courthouse or voice

box or courage

Didn't believe in a man whose reputation relied on grooming children
So I went to Oz hoping to find all three of Dorothy's wishes, but never home
I never wanted to go home where everyone could find me, whether I wanted them to or not.

I never tried to break it apart, so I left all my purchases behind and thought of becoming a runaway
Only the road always ended with hopelessness
trails of my blood lining doorsteps like the twelfth plague of Israel

I wonder if all first daughters have some curse thrusted upon them
And hope, whether great or small, is the most dangerous thing I've ever owned
'Cause I used to believe in Santa Claus until I didn't
and I imagined my success through every autobiography that made me think that I could be a new generation of Marguerite Johnson.

I used to believe in Santa Claus, used to believe in Christmas
Used to believe in joy and happiness, and now.
Now I don't know what I believe, just that none of these things are on my list anymore
and most days, I pray for the return of my innocence.

4 *"If I were a different kind of person, I might say this whole incident is a metaphor for life in general: things get broken, and sometimes they get repaired, and in most cases, you realize that no matter what gets damaged, life rearranges itself to compensate for your loss, sometimes wonderfully."* (Harold Stein) ~ Hanya Yanagihara, A Little Life

Recipe for childhood haints

uniform tunic, blouse, marino bra, tights, panty
grown man's fingers stripping slowly down

tears
protests
dirty layers of embarrassment caked over already
thick skin
eyes crossed,
closed,
bleeding
just waiting for it to end.
for the night to stop sneaking a grown man into the bed
sheets of a child.

Bows,
ribbons,
bubbles,
banana clips,
clips,
Mickey Mouse hairstyles
Anything to make them see that puberty doesn't mean
maturity

razors,
pins,
needles,
knifes,
sharp edges
drawing blood so they understand that what they do has

a consequence as valuable as life

Pills
Cigarettes
Alcohol
Pills
Pills
Pills
Measuring your choices near the rising of your chest
weighing how much it would take to draw your
final breath

flatlines
defibrillators
stomach pumps
Death?

Who am I to blame her for breaking past the fixtures of
sexual abuse in her gene?
Who am I to pay her debts instead of helping her to
tear open these generational curses with crucifixes of
tongues turned every witch way but right-side
to Jerusalem?
and the fairy godmother takes all the credit for her
healing,takes all the Palo Mayombe that drives us to learn
what lies beyond ritual
and insanity.

Takes all the morality and magic and calls it blessed.
Calls forgiveness without amnesia a hologram that can't
bleed onto anything else.
Call me a replica of a child she used to know.

Call bitterness a sick song plaited into the tragedies of
Prospero's smile.
Call oceans and beach breeze death traps for fantasy.
Call me malicious for blowing abengs to study ledgers of
ill-suffered women in history.

But who am I to blame her for draining herself white to
escape the story written for her?
Dear oxygen mask of a skin, that I occasionally tell the
mirror is pretty,
How do I balance out the carbon monoxide of my self-
hate before I begin to see my own impurity tied around
the maypole in the ribbons of a baby's innocence?

Triggers

Motions argued by criminal justice students have posed questions dehumanizing the effect of a rape kit and the statute of limitations on each body aggressively melting itself onto another without so much as a reasonable doubt to obtain a search warrant for the dormant weapons of the thighs.

They further claim that the statute of limitations for a crime is nothing but a safety net for the bitter to launch premeditated attacks on the ships of the comfortable, as if the ammunition birthed from trauma and adopted into their brain was nothing more than security for blackmail.

They say these people who prosecute after the death of a crime have ill intentions, so they shouldn't be taken seriously. Sometimes they degrade the experience because it wasn't within their perceived time frame, or the perpetrator was too upstanding a citizen to be labeled as predator.

I guess this is how well the law serves us; guess the expiration date on justice isn't flexible enough to safeguard the interests of the fearful who choose to bleed on the tapestries of anyone who can stomach the gory details of their failure as women.

To the people who force these arguments down the throats of survivors who have been frozen in time,
How do you still close your eyes in prayer and ask God to

forgive your crimes?

What if he said that the statute of limitations on your sin had expired and that your mistake would cost you your life, making you live in fear of every waking moment?

What if you didn't walk but stood in their shoes, facing the backlash from people who could never understand how intrusive it feels to have medical exams? I argue that sometimes these questions seek to serve as triggers, or rather, to find them.

So I went searching for mystery boxes and found a few more that will never get easier,
but someone said to have faith like the mustard seed, and I'm still trying to be able to locate that peace, but I've figured that it's mighty hard to do when you're sitting in the stirrups, making way for lighted scapulas to take cells from you as if you haven't already felt like you've lost enough.

It's not the physical pain that hurts as much as the memories that come flooding back and the sharp screams inside from the broken girl whose bones refuse to stay buried.

Sometimes those screams erupt from the volcano of lungs into the streams of pillows, not able to console them.

It's not my fault that I'm a woman, but it's my fault for having tests that would trigger how violated I would feel knowing that I'm still nursing this blood on the hem of my dress without even attempting to heal.

I thought this rope reeling me in would stop by now,
and I thought that when I prayed, God would turn on his
hearing aid, but I guess I placed too much trust in a supreme
being I'm still unable to see, and I can't break myself out of
the pattern of trusting him because maybe Christianity is
real, and maybe if I wait long enough, like Hannah, Eli won't
see me as mad, but pray with me
because if the saints petition for you, then the Lord will see
that somehow, in reigning in lost sheep, he forgot that I still
got my horns caught in the Genesis weeds for sacrifice.

I'm starting to believe that maybe this is my fault, but I've
been so focused on passing the blame around like a game.

I don't think this is the Lord's doing, but the devil has too
many sins on his plate that aren't his for me to try and hide
my misgivings under his mattress.

I'm woman, and that means I should be strong, so I'll fight,
and if I lose, then it was worth the shot.

She becomes church mouse, with an inevitable bliss for quietness

and solace
becomes markings of the past
she doesn't want to draw attention but how can she live if
her heart no longer beats,
if her skin is no longer home
if her brain sends bat signals to God and whispers of
beauty and modesty and death
a warrior princess like Xena squandering her rebellions
as a bloodlust of crude memory

She becomes a church mouse, keeping all her thoughts
close to her chest so no one can hurt her

X things they never tell you about the daughters of a molester

After Siaara Freeman's 'X Things they never told you about the drug dealer's daughter

I.   She is the consequence of what was supposed to be love or lust; a bundle of joy rocked in the bassinet that was his arms as he promised to always offer God guidance and protection. The molester's first victims were the sheltered daughters, who never knew that danger could be synonymous to protection.[5]

II.   When she first hears a catcall, it triggers alarm bells in her body, and her shrewdness is directed at the man calling out to her, thinking that she is beautiful enough to be acquainted with his anatomy. And when he offers lewd words about her sexiness, she hears the orders of her father, and she knows she will never be entirely comfortable in a world that has more predators than protectors. Because of this, she starts to second-guess all her clothing and actions, praying that what she does and wears does not trigger the devil in anyone else.

III.   She is the reincarnation of Hercules. And by the time she meets her hydra, she is too consumed by fear to locate her strength. So she distances herself from the world around her in preparation for her own Titanomachy.

IV.   They do not tell you that the day she decided to be

5 *"The truth is everyone will hurt you. You just have to find the ones worth suffering for." ~ Bob Marley*

an artist, her first masterpiece had long since chiseled itself into flesh, so that with every drop of blood, she is powerful enough to abracadabra her magic back from Mexico.[6]

V.   By the time she has friends, she has learned to compartmentalize her life into fractions of her identity. When her war is over, she forgets where she had placed anything but anger and resentment.

VI.   She learns to love religion and history, hoping that somewhere in the oldest stories, she may find the right tool to kill a contemporary hydra who drew power from trapping her in the closets, and when she finally learns that her trips to Mexico will not stop, she begins to question God about the plans Jeremiah claimed he had for her life, so she constantly loses faith yet still hopes that God will come save her from the road of destruction littering her sight.

VII.   She does not tell you that the first time her father preys, it is over her older sisters, whose mouths were sewed shut for fear of losing the father figure they have earned, because the only time his love holds their hand is to squeeze it into submission for his approval.

VIII.   The first time she woke to him on his knees searching the greenhouse of her youth, he had already learned to ruffle through the budding plants of flowers he never cared for, flowers whose names she had no recollection of,

6 Alludes to the children's game, "I don't want to go to Mexico, no, more, more, there's a big fat policeman at the door. He will grab you by the collar and make you pay a dollar..." Despite several meanings attached to the game, I use it to mean one of the more common ones, which is about sexual abuse.

and she finally learned the meaning of growth. So much so that she learns that horror stories are only comedies for the broken.

IX.   Before she is a known statistic, she watches the mist of regret crush the places she loves, and the people she knows regard her with pity as if she is the cause of all that has happened. The girl, her sister, and her brothers move on with their lives, hoping that they can walk away from whoever knew that the closed doors of their home were not always safe, only private islands filled with contemporary prideful criminals brainwashing those under their thumb with financial security and family. And by now she has grown so bitter that she decides that all families are better off without male figures, so she weaponizes the machete of her tongue to help those like her as she becomes unnecessarily critical and unjustified in her judgment of every adult.

X.   By the time she learns to stop hiding from her truth, she is already too ashamed of daily doses of sexual crimes on the news because she knows that somewhere, every report never made is one more criminal left out, and that means that there is another line of victims she unintentionally has a hand in creating.

X.   She has dissected the parts of her that somehow tie her spirit to his, but by the time the deeds of the closet in his room come to the altar, the wildfire of her nightmare travels across all four oceans like slave ships distributing chaos, so she makes a ritual of setting her sails far away for fear that she once again houses the side effect of the statistic that is depression.

X.   The girl loses the magic of Hercules when she loses the art that kept her sane; she loses her magic when she forgets empathy and cries each night; she loses her magic when she forgets how to write and is placed on pills not meant to make her forget but to make her less angry at herself. She has lost her magic but has recovered her love for reading and movies because a land of fantasy means she can manipulate her own happy ending.

X.   When she reappears in her old playground, she cloaks herself in the uniform it first happened in, walks the same grounds that sheltered girl did, and sets the stakes on how long this 19-year-old can stomach racing through towns and people she was once close with. She sees old friends who reiterate that she was never to run, for they do not see the filth on her that she still cannot wash off. They highlight that she is still loved no matter the distance or the time, and she prays that one day she will learn to believe that even a quarter of it is the truth.

X.   She holds onto the reins of her sanity like it is a wishbone or a lifeline to better days.

X.   I know the molester's daughter is nothing more than a myth, incorporated into smoke rising into the air to clog the throats of anyone coming too close to uprooting *her truth. That her trips to Mexico were daily, and her shame at herself kept her nearer to death than it did heaven. I know that all Greek gods were molesters, rapists, and fanatics, and this world is not large enough to dissipate sexual criminals if the media propagates such horrendousness as kinks and all mythologies shape-shift each relevance into demigods doing good, but does that make it less of a crime if the women and men are tricked into a false sense of security by people they feel they knew? They say sometimes Greek gods are bored, and the Romans followed suit, leading to the art Lucretia's body made, but now we have a set of people who think it's right, forgetting that all abused have the power of most goddesses with the blood magic inherited from the sacrifice of Lucretia. I hope they know that her wrist was cut for those who may never find their own magic.*

When they say all things are either black or white

I say I don't believe in the inerrant principles of yin and
yang
I believe, however, in the hidden trauma of life after
fundamentalism
I believe it is bullshit enough to counteract the fuel
of Dionysus through my blood when I want to dilute
oxygen and forget how to breathe without hands-on
asphyxiation or suffocation

I believe that if I survive surviving, then I am not strong.
I am just stupid enough to not have died and I wonder
why God never made life easy
Why he had to have so many answers from people who
have never had to ask him any of the hard questions

I want to ask him how come some people get the
fairytale and some of us wish our tears could mutate into
a painting Picasso would be proud of
Mutate into some kind of blood-ridden rainbow or wind
chime or hope steeling itself into their homes

And they whisper that children shouldn't have to know
how to write like this
Instead of saying children shouldn't have to practice the
laugh of Bruce when they watch Dory
Or that
pain shouldn't have to make them annoyed at those who
say that everyone has life hard

and everything in life is quick
And it's so fleeting that I wonder why it never takes me
but goes slowly by
And
Everything in life is some demented joke

Is some crime scene waiting to happen, whether in my
head, on paper, or here on this green earth he said was
wonderful

And I never have the answers I am looking for

And I want to tell everyone searching for them that it
gets better, but I'm still convincing myself that it does

I still tell my mind it's in the past, and there is no physical
scar there to make it torment me occasionally.
And I want to tell everyone to fight to prevent it
To make sure it never happens
To close their eyes and see rainbows and harps and
something happy so it doesn't become a permanent
bleed, a permanent tattoo, or an ill-written
summary of yourself
An x-ray carved in the ethmoid and sphenoid of someone
else who shouldn't have had that sort of clearance
anyway.

And I want to tell them to keep it
Tell them those parts change over time
Tell them to hold onto their healing

Tell them to walk away from that chamber in their head
and never ever return

When they start questioning God, I want to tell them that
He doesn't answer when they want Him to, and sometimes
we cry over His reply without seeing His hands move in our
favor. I'm still learning that.

CHAPTER II
Deranged

Susanna Kaysen:

"People ask, 'how did you get in there?' What they really want to know is if they are likely to end up there as well. I can't answer the real question. All I can tell them is, 'it's easy.' And it is easy to slip into a parallel universe. Most people pass over incrementally, making a series of perforations in the membrane between here and there until an opening exists. And who can resist an opening?"

~ Girl Interrupted (1999)[7]

---

7 "Normality is a paved road: It's comfortable to walk, but no flowers grow on it." ~ Vincent Van Gogh

What if I become so afraid of my mind that I start to fight back?

What if my mind becomes a maze I am unable to escape?
What if my mind becomes a permanent escape tunnel
that shelters me from reality?[8]
What if that escape becomes a curse?
What if my mind becomes a curse or shade like my skin
on concrete? What if I saw how my brain looked spilled
over into tombstones that I could not cross?
What if my mind becomes a tombstone and drowns a
church?
Becomes bloated spleens and belt buckles with no
purpose.
Becomes criminal because it is black?
and trapped becomes whistleblowing sirens and Pitbull
attacks?

What if my mind sees cacti multiplying on its surface?
What if my mind becomes a cloned version of Devon
Wright's thoughts? becomes a fall, so severe ballads are
written in tribute to its darkness,
as if I am the fame Marilyn warned of,
as if I am Cleo's sacrifice,
as if I am Susanna Kaysen,
as if I am Poussey never making it to the finishing credits.

What if my mind becomes ouroboros?
or it becomes me,
or I become my mind,

8 *"A question that sometimes drives me hazy: am i or the others crazy?"*
~ Albert Einstein

or my identity is self-sufficient on what I store in
between its locks.

Sometimes I fear the things that go on in my mind
because it was never meant to hold
so many terrible destinies.

Conversation with anxiety

I learned a few lessons while laughing and talking to myself.
The first is that depression is a dead-end road.

You see, my depression says she doesn't do the morning
thing. She browses through the gram in the afternoon, but
her legs don't work, so she lays on her back most of the day.

My anxiety says she's just a freeloader.
having everything handed to her while playing tricks like
she's Swiper stealing from Dora

My anxiety says my depression is a narcissistic bitch who
doesn't know when she's wronged someone. I asked if she
had ever wronged me. She didn't respond.
but I knew it was because my anxiety never ceases to speak
if she won't hear her own voice. She too is a self-centered
bitch that's
set in her ways, trying to get me to embrace her actions,
and she rattles on about what my depression does and
doesn't do. Painting a picture that can't be true, she said.

My depression plays with the weather of my emotions,
convincing me that this is the type of work I deserve to do.

See
My depression determines whether I starve or eat frozen
dinners alone when she gets tired of spinning me in Mad
Hatter's teacup.

My anxiety says that's her way of knowing that she can still control me. It seems my depression gets off on
punishing me.
to feed her ego.

My anxiety says I keep her around because I'm fearful of having to survive every day in the unknown
My anxiety says that my depression has manifested itself into a poet, so when I stay too long in her embrace, I too become a poem. My world turned upside down so that a stranger could assess how deep the storyline goes.

My anxiety says there is rarely a plot twist because, like poets, my poison ivy anchors me to the misfits and gives me bars so thick an acupuncturist needle couldn't fit through.

My anxiety says she thinks my depression is just afraid of me becoming a chiropractor and resetting my bones in place so that I can unpack all my issues in front of people with an appetite for destruction.

My anxiety says that my depression loves to hear me recite my story like Shakespearean lines in the middle of an encore.

So I swung at her and missed
She laughed heartily and said that this isn't new.
I'm just a weak link, and there isn't a move I can make that she hasn't seen before. It turns out I outplayed my hand 27 lifetimes ago.

My anxiety had a blacksmith signet the tools to pluck my strings like slave cotton.

My depression says
She's a fighter and hasn't yet met her match because there is not a king powerful enough to throw down or run his gauntlet.

I closed my eyes, clasped my hands, and tried to use my only escape out of this maze, but the women on my shoulders tell me that I've forgotten my roots while embracing falsified European truths. And here I was thinking
that I was doing this prayer thing right. And that, like a hippopotamus, my prayers weighed more than a simple ton. But

My prayers and my mind were just like a simpleton's. I found out that my anxiety loves gambling.
She's a debtor, robbing Peter to pay Paul. And that's how she ended up in
Depression's net in the first place, and they are still as thick as thieves, the best of friends, and enemies to boot.

She said I'd never find a friend that loyal, so I should stop looking, but I am consistent in my persistence, so I don't have to see them deflecting. My depression says she has used anxiety to strike strong men before prancing naked and blindsiding them with the hated truth that she is the embodiment of their deepest fears.

My anxiety says she has no shame in her game, and I shouldn't take it personally when she's a symptom of every death; just check her Wikipedia page.

When I started writing this, my depression said that she's an activist and a feminist supporting all rights, but she's gender fluid, and I should stop referring to her as a woman or man. When I don't know what she has hidden beneath her breeches, and I guess I should understand because misidentification is a sorry hand,
stealing individualism and her sense of control.

And pardon me because I realize I'm doing it again, but to hell with it because since she took over, I found myself stuck in a no-win situation just like the soldiers in Afghanistan: kill or be killed, but you'd still have the trauma on your hands.

And I became complacent because my depression didn't come embedded with a manual,
But if you find the kill switch, let me know because this machine is running out of fuel.

My depression says she kicks like a mule now and again just to prove to me that torment isn't the only discomfort or pain I can feel. She says she hits snooze for me daily, and when I chastise her for being lazy, she leans back like her job is done. Isn't that crazy?

My depression got me feeling like that cousin no one knows at the family cookout.

It got me anticipating questions and imagining scenarios that I wouldn't ever be in.

My anxiety got my breath coming up short in cardiac arrest, and she used panic to nurture me into scaling fences to avoid danger, just to be afraid of anything that wasn't empty, dark, and cold.

My depression says she isn't sad, but he's a prime factor in her quadratic equation.

My anxiety says they are the first stem scholars because to be this successful as entrepreneurs, I've got to know when to tip the scales.

My depression said she's ready for the next round, saying it's not improbable that she can humiliate me.
She does it regularly, and my depression can't take the blame for most of my actions, though she'd like to.
And if her words didn't cut so deep, where would I be?

Because when she comes to stay, she stays a while, and my brain says to take her absence and celebrate it instead of worrying about when she'll be back.
But my anxiety casts a bet, saying that my engine will always refuse to move in fear that I can't find a groove.

She says the world outside is cruel, and I have to protect myself from the shelter in here.
But it won't be so easy to be safe from her when I won't survive without her company.

See,
My depression is attached to me, and it's all because I take steps back into the shadows where no sniper can get close enough to break me free.[9]

9 *Life is an enigma that is always better a little deranged.*

To be happy

For once, I imagine that his eyes were not familiar with redness.

That he wouldn't visit the sea so often to wash his face in pain. I wished the walls of many halls and bathroom floors wouldn't know the multiple times he held his hands in fists, and attacked them for things they never did.

How many times should his mouth go wide with screams that refuse to erupt?

How many times should his hands claw at his head, wishing the voices would just shut up?

And it hasn't been once or twice that he's tried to mute his uneasy mind. I constantly pray that his pillow didn't have to worry about wiping tears or struggle through the fear of drowning darkness submerged beneath crystal waterfalls. I wished his lips didn't know lies with upward curls and words wouldn't constantly echo in his ear.

I wish I could ease your pain, little boy.
I wish the world could see the scars that make you worth it. I wish I had caught you before you fell.
I wish I was there in time to hold you back when you jumped. And I still remember my arms outstretched, my voice screaming. But wasn't I a hypocrite

Two broken souls, each trying to keep the other alive, and isn't it beautiful how we both sought the same peace?

But if you had left, would I still regard death as peace, or would it just mean the promise of reuniting with my heart's missing piece?

Whatever it may be, know that we are both strong.
If we ever needed each other, I believe it was when we both made an appointment six feet under.

I've heard that blood ties that dabble in friendships are oftentimes stronger. So, may our mental health rest in peace, little brother.[10]

10 *For my brother, written July 2018.*

Imagine, depression is funny like that

Imagine lying awake with tears streaming down your face.
Drowning in guilt with no idea what you supposedly did.
Watching those blurred corners of your room come caving
in on you.
Still unable to move,
Too, mesmerized by the beckoning darkness, or rather a
darkness that sings failure like a siren. Your failures.

Never mind that you are driving down a rocky street,
blindfolded yet somehow staring back.

And you know this can't be right. You're supposed to be
awake in bed. Because that's what I just said.
[11]Imagine trying to stifle the voices urging you to
pull at your hair. To scream
to silence your thoughts so that they, whoever they are, can
speak. Imagine not being able to tell anyone.
To scream To shout

Imagine being told to smile more, laugh even. Because
depression isn't for kids, you're only
sad. Imagine holding on to faith because someone said it
would be better with a couple of funny videos.

You tell them, You feel sick.
You tell them, You're tired.
You tell them, You're going mad hearing voices that just
won't shut up. Voices that sound too much like your own,

---

11 "There are times when the mind is dealt such a blow it hides itself in
insanity. While this may not seem beneficial, it is. There are times when
reality is nothing but pain, and to escape that pain the mind must leave
reality behind" ~ Patrick Rothfuss

annoying as old chalk scraping on a blackboard.
You beg them to ease the pain.

Imagine not being able to take it anymore. Watch them
smile and call you a tad dramatic.
Someone in need of relaxation

Understand that anyone who has never walked these dark
roads will never recognize that there is no manual for
depression. No one to guide you out of the maze and
lead you home.
Imagine complaining of pain so often that your body has
been pricked more times than a voodoo doll. The only thing
left is to be cut open and your organs pulled inside out to
find the source of pain.

But depression has already diagnosed that you're a danger
to yourself. Depression is funny that way.

It takes all the attention off itself to blame you for things
you never did. Sometimes, I wonder if my paralysis is from
fear or fascination.

My breath hitched in my throat. My heart racing because
I have no bones to keep this sack of flesh from crashing.
During those hours, it's as if my body lays in bed. My bones
at the gates of hell. My mind buried in an unmarked grave
deep within the forest of my past. A cemetery where the
guards are monsters resembling... myself?

That's the funny thing about depression. It makes you feel as if you are your own tormentor.
And
I watch it all. Unable to move. Unable to scream.
Silenced by fevered kisses, I pray may linger.

They remind me of my happy days. Days where I think I am healthy, and this short virus has done its course like a cold I could never regain. On those days, I smile and laugh, for the hallowed-eyed girl cannot be found. I flirt and blush because my heart is not controlled.
I do have happy days.

Then there are days when storm clouds rage. I am force-fed pills upon pills with a bottle to the head.
On those days, I feel like a helpless wife.
Battered and bruised by an aristocratic husband with too much power to be charged, and I contemplate ending us both. Because I'd rather be dead.

On those days, I cry for hours until I'm numb because I cannot deal with the gaze.
On those days,
I formulate so many excuses that I start believing
they are true.
There are days I want to be alone.
Days I push people away and don't care if they ever return.
Days where I'm too tired to explain that I have no appetite.
Or why I prefer to stick my finger down my throat.
Too tired to explain my overeating because I'm already in

a crowd too noisy for my liking.

So, I isolate myself.
What can I say?
Everyone knows I'm antisocial.
But both days, happy or sad, I know I have no one to turn to.

My therapist said it's natural. All men feel pain.
I don't think she understands that my pain isn't seen as real
by family and friends. Teachers must think I'm delinquent.
And the church probably just sees a sinner who is not good
enough for repentance.
She stirs up too many memories.
Digging up rotting corpses buried too long and too far, that
I had already forgotten they existed.

She calls it trauma therapy, but I believe she uses them to
make me feel belittled. She says it helps build my character.

My therapist is a mortician.
My therapist is my anxiety.
My therapist acts like a friend because she doesn't like to
share me with depression.

It's been years.
And I'm still going 900,000 miles without headlights.
A rear-view mirror as my main sight.
There are no signs along this bumpy road, this town
resembling the mists of time long forgotten. Times when
I was my happiest.

I guess it's time I realized that, I've spiraled too far out of control, for
Depression is now me, and anxiety is my lover.

The one where I write my own healing

You asked if I would like to be buried here.
But I think I'd like to go
far away from those who have ever had the displeasure of
knowing me.

So,
Scatter me with jungles, mountains, and desserts.
Burn my essence so they may not haunt me, for how could
someone who has never survived request a burial in a place
where their memory never lived?

coat me in depression

palletize a casket worth the pain for I've been here before.
Swallowed more salt from tears than I do water

Trekking this failure of womanhood into my skin like
needlepoint pleasure, scattering fragments of my soul far
away

[12]Consistently wondering how death would feel extracted
from my lungs like a possession I ingest from bottled spirits
in my weakness.

And if I should die tomorrow, let my last hours be as I had
practiced
May death be on time to pick me up, dressed in pink and
flaunting all the beauty that's so hard to see through fear.

---

12 Rose Kennedy once said, "Birds sing after a storm; why shouldn't people
feel as free to delight in whatever sunlight remains to them?"

Remember when I romanticized suicide?

Remember when I became the accelerated hijack of her beliefs?
When I hung onto the perfection of the Lisbon sisters?

I was a Black girl whose victimology disintegrated within 24 hours.
A Black girl pickpocketing the dissertations of her mother's half-empty memoir and the conjecture of her father's calloused crafts blended them together, forming corrosive substances for gene editing.

A reconstruction that does not make me better than the girl I used to be. Only unidentifiable to the torments and hopes that no longer chase after me.

I romanticized suicide.

committed myself by tying belt notches around the bedpost of my throat wishing I had the courage to squeeze harder each time I heard the pumping drawing me deeper into an embrace so many know

And I saw that suicide, too, was a Black girl becoming a pioneer in her own assaults.
A Black girl who became unhinged and devolved choosing to tie her identity to the stories of Shahrazade and the illustrated man.

I became suicide, born again to be an organized and functioning alcoholic, mixing bromine to wash my skin of the domestic secrets these suburban bricks hold.

My therapist said

When another unimaginative ideation skitters across the
pedestrian walkways of my mind I should put the pen down
instead of replacing it.
Draw in a breath and say to the night stars I am done

Yes, I'm a quitter. You can pin that on my chest.Let it be my
scarlet letter because it kept me alive and grounded so far.
And so far this pen has left me few regrets.

When young

I battled the storm with silent resilience
and called it strength
stuffed a wadded-up newspaper
in the outhouse of my mouth
curled my tongue around sea anemones and stifled the
aftershock that was far from perfect

I became reliant on never becoming an Indian paintbrush

[13]I'm older but still clamping down on every emotion that
keeps attacking
I believe that I have learned how to tackle anything

But sometimes, these tears find a niche in my armor,
and I cry at the fall of a pen before I do major events. It's
funny how much of an artichoke I've become.
Peeling back layers to see what pain makes me surrender.

13 *The Indian paintbrush as referenced here is one of the many names given
to the parasitic flower more widely known as Castilleja*

CHAPTER III
Memento Mori

Julius Caesar:

"A coward dies a thousand times before his death, but the valiant taste of death but once. It seems to me most strange that men should fear, seeing that death, a necessary end, will come when it will come."

There is a sort of virtue within dying, that makes death before dishonor a mantra worth believing.

For my friend's mother[14]

When my friend's mother died, I cried because it was the first time I knew that the mind could swallow you whole, even if you look like you have it all on the outside.

While fighting dragons with the faces of bronze gargoyles, no one cares to see behind your smiles.
Because she made me know that there were people like me propped up on depression's box and hiding anxiety while taking care of those around her, I became woman, brazen, and loud with my faults, with my thoughts, and with the things that hide in the dark.

I spoke up and I moved out.

When I heard the news, I learned that hugs were not teddy bear kisses or warm summers along a surfers beach; they were not heartfelt, but a prototype for CIA torture methods rained on the daughters who were tired of hearing condolences and well wishes from people they may never see or hear from again.

And news of her death sounded like the silence of slaughtered lambs. Like entrapments marching through the tomb of Lazarus that took bathroom breaks and truck stops on the half of their hearts, each donated and surgically melted together to make well on the omen that was their mother's death, all so they could each bury part of her in a church that locked her on the outside.

And
Hugs became like eggshells breaking at the reactions
from people refusing to move on from the electrocution
of the facts, that schoolmates and friends would never be
mature enough to come up with the right words to say to
her daughters, who never should have had the hiccups of
death chiming beneath their choked sentences that young.

And I remembered her fondly, remember her bleached hair
and gentle smile as she sat waiting for school to get out,
how she was so involved and something never made much
sense to me so I wonder if when she looks onto the gray
of the horizon did she ever see her own body playing host
to the unknown equations the living have no knowledge
of and I wonder if the lifeless shade became her favorite
color wonder if it was the peace that set her at ease in her
last hours watching Elijah's chariot in thunderstorms and
somehow I knew that patience would become the attribute
my friend would work on 'cause nothing would be the same
if the gramoxone in her mother's stomach had pumped
itself into the brain of the crowd praying for her survival
the crowd hugging her daughters like they were runaways
like they were criminals trying to catch the stars instead of
moving out from under the collapse of the sky.

Now I watch her, no longer 15, try to conjure up her mother's
ghost in every dream she chases and every Mother's Day
promise. I watch her project the notions that will someday
force her to steeple over herself like origami eagles without
wings to keep her last promise and take care of the girl no

longer 8 who never left her side but bled with her.

And I thank God that she still has a support system that never leaves her back unattended to be broken or stabbed, and I think about what a great legacy a mother can leave behind for her daughters when she cannot leave herself.

How great a person these daughters become after becoming all they dare and making mistakes to learn from themselves. And she must be proud of all they have accomplished because they are the finest treasures she ever left behind the day she thought they were ready to each become their sister's keeper.

14 *"I once heard an elder say that the dead who have no use for their words leave them as part of their children's inheritance. Proverbs, teeth suckings, obscenities, even grunts and moans once inserted in special places during conversations, all are passed along to the next heir." ~ Edwidge Danticat, The Farming of Bones*

X *truths about suicide*

I.   *The truth about attempting suicide is that it becomes as casual as selectively choosing toys from department store aisles; it becomes routine as pinning iron pendulums on bulletin boards seeking hitmen from homicidal maniacs as if the ripcord imploding in us is the unbalanced nostalgia of thrift store coffee, old books, and porch swings when waves crash against the bank on a sunset beach.*

II.   *They never tell you that the churning of allegiance to the sporadic nerves inside your chest rewrites the inevitability of sharp razors, of doctors cutting through ligature marks to find a pulse, or just somewhere to push IV lines.*

III.   *The truth about suicide is that it worms its way into suburban picket fences too, leaking gas into confined steel, poaching men and women as the fuzz lurches embers of fury we have clutched at straws to quench, and we can no longer diffuse it, when it becomes embedded in the walls of our homes.*

IV.   [15]*The truth about suicide is that it is a condescending thread of duct tape and a ball of kitty toys unearthed by solitary torches in vacant chimney sweeps. Wrapping itself around our throats strangling the words we may utter to exorcise it from our doorsteps.*

---

15 *"Our society is so adamant about making a point that you have to get better quickly--instant gratification--or you have to act like you're at least better quickly. And you don't. It's okay to act like you're not okay for that time being. But as long as you get out of it and get there and take your time and do what you need, that's all that matters." ~ Elijah, Spectrum Suicide Survivors*

V.   The truth about suicide is that when you die, they finally uncover the blind spots in their memory and find out that your silence and this act are a logical reaction to your mind backfiring so many times.

VI.   The truth about suicide is that it becomes another bedlam, another flicker of steam encapsulated within wax falling over the coats of pupils aligned with the blank canvas of life snuffed out.

VII.   The truth about suicide is that the spills of blood cauterize themselves to form hangers for closet coats.

VIII.   The truth about suicide is that it is not selfish, is not a statement, is not memorialized, and is not just a minimal statistic.

IX.   The truth about suicide is that it is an ode to frustrated days, an ode to veins sparkling outside like Halloween candy, like unselfishness, like survival, like mummification, like the perseverance of memory.

X.   The truth about suicide is that it is a back alley to death, to freedom, to hope, to salvation, a crowbar to the pessimistic belief of the self-proclaimed saints, and it becomes a matter of how you choose to see it.

X.   The truth about suicide is that you stand at your own wake with bated breath for the day they finally say Suicide is a virtue long lost in the propaganda of the story that unselfish suicide is unassisted euthanasia, and ain't she great at it.

X.   The truth about suicide is that it is forever a southern belle filled with eulogies and great memories that we choose to keep.

X.   The truth about suicide is that she is not selfish, just a misunderstood wrecking ball catapulted by cranes of adrenaline fashioned from the harness of fight,freeze, fawn because the truth is that not every disappointment begins with a goodbye lesson.

X.   Maybe if I say it loud enough or long enough, it will change the outcome of the stereotype. SUICIDE IS NOT SELFISH. She is the best hello with a halo; a goodbye seated in white robes.

X.   Sometimes, the truth about suicide is that we do not know when it stops being unselfish.

X.   We forget that suicide is not selfish, just what to call a traumatic act that we cannot understand, only to put a negative connotation on an emotional sounding board for wounds.

X.   The truth is, I know nothing of suicide, just her Ideations and the bad days that break us down.

X.   The truth about suicidal attempts is that they

soon break free from their cocoons and become suicidal butterflies.

X.   The truth about what happens after suicidal attempts is unselfish, for there is no virtue in forcing life on someone longing for death, all because you cannot see the strength in letting them go.

The first time I knew death to be permanent

was when I watched her place chrysanthemums on the lungs of a woman who raised me with nothing but oxygen-infused love. It was my first introduction to the fragility of life,
into knowing how it feels to want to save someone when you know you won't be able to

it was my first encounter with something fickle
and permanent, and I told myself I would not cry, would not forget her

now it's seven years later since December 27, and my memories are scarce

Because I had time to make them as a child but never time to be of an age where I can have a relationship surpassing respect and sole discipline with her without blurring the lines.

the second time death knocked close to home was the day my brother caught her peeping

found out she came courting another woman who raised us

She showed herself to him as a curtain call, proving how subtle she

could dismantle a working kidney or fog the sight
when in the throes of the living we don't understand how
much of a bully she can be when she's got a target.

We couldn't beat her with our ill understanding of her
and our efforts to help in the fight.

And we froze this time, unable to cry should she think us
predictable in this tyranny.

The third time she came calling I was old enough to expect
her had already lost the bond anchoring me with the third
woman who grew me. So I didn't cry, but I was still paralyzed
in shock, nursing an eerie feeling I could not understand so
I searched through books, hoping to find an answer that
wouldn't metastasize into the mess her family untangled
as the truth as they all but Bible-thumped this delerance
duppy from her roots, proving that, as humans, we all have
stupid things that grief and fear of the unknown make us do.

She came for three women who grew me, looked another
in her eyes and said,
"you next"
intermixed herself into sickness, double dosed her body
with thyroids
Rocked her bones like they be cradles of dynamite should
she shift the wrong way then it's no coming back and she
fought
Gave it all she had,
this woman fought illness back so much so I respect her

for that.

I saw death come for three women who raised me,
[16]Left the fourth a shadow of herself, not that we
really noticed
but I saw death hold trophies like the power of serial killer
souvenirs first a lung
Watched her ambitions push her towards grabbing hold of
sight and a kidney
Then an entire body
and I wonder who else she'll take before she gets tired of
lingering by my doorstep for criminals always learn to add
to their kills and their trophies.

16 *For 4 women who had a hand in raising me (daily, weekends, holidays, etc.):*

Doreen Waugh-Fagan (Cancer warrior, R.I.P.)
Juliet Bailey (Kidney failure, R.I.P.)
Pam Henry (Cancer warrior, R.I.P.)
Nadine Gordon-Davis thanks for all you did

I blew my lungs out with the hookah last night

held it up to the sky and wondered how black was too
black, thought to pour the whites cascading down my
liver into her cavities
like this poison be gospel,
be a testimony purified and filtered
be a prophecy of peace twenty packs a piece
like I could mulatto muddle melanated menthol medicine
marinated for years to be another Tuskegee error Black
men swear to die by
Be another great stress revolver aimed at our necks while
we ignore our pleas that we can't breathe
that this smell radiating off us be another enforcer for
radiation treatments
be another panpipe profit pilot protruding pyrolysis from
bank statements that still don't make sense,
A disease that got us paying for death like she ain't the
one lucky to be graced with all this melanin
like she ain't lucky enough to kiss the lips of a pharaoh or
a goddess
or just someone who wears this skin so goddamn high
our own lungs get jealous, and my cousin says she cannot
stop
that this chokehold gets tight enough to edge her to
heaven, that this edging makes her remember she is still
living so she blows through a pack daily
counting her 70-odd years in the ringlets toward the
heavens, not caring if this is sickness or relief,
somehow, it no longer matters

and she doesn't know when it stopped being anything
only that the pipes came when she needed them
only that they have been her backbone and sole
comforter for years she has forgotten how to be
independent
has forgotten how to be anything but black and mild,
forgotten her own definition when her wallet, Micheal
Jackson, moonwalks itself into bars for both baptism and
retort, shedding sagging flesh not worth induction into
the rapture
and she says she cannot see where her money goes as
she slams a six on the table and puffs another Craven A
knowing that somewhere between British companies and
American drinks, she finds a shortcut to fulfilling six-foot
house plans, which she dutifully lays.

Now her most captivating art piece threatens to hang
itself on the walls of her future home white liver black
lungs a contrast to the poison in her blood.

Emblazon their memories; say their names

After the continuous execution of Black men and women.
Written for Sonya Massey and others before and after her.

Another name got added to the list coxing another Canaan walk in concrete jungles avoiding predators protecting interests unknown

bullets spraying for threats body cams won't show us; another spin on a narrative that can't be real another name stripped from a mother to be revised as a hashtag; a tabloid of some news washed over until another name makes the headlines, yet we never forgot when our soles bore the strains of the last bullet tearing through threats conceived by prejudice

another popular story stripping any form of privacy from families grieving "God why?"

another prayer ushered up to heaven when the heart cannot bear its own weight anymore

another obituary fading into statistics, animated eulogies on courtroom pews professing pleas for less time

another guilty verdict jaywalks another badge through these streets because probable cause can be twisted if the altercation isn't recorded,

and force is justified when the life of the killer is presumed at risk, but if dead men tell no tales that's the side of the story no one misses except for those seeing this world from different lenses

and this reality is nothing but another reason to say "thank you for your service" while praying it's not a statement that will cost you another reason to deny or hesitate the request of an entry without warrant because of fear that you will remember the wrong names on new faces with the same objective, praying that these encounters doesn't leave your name a misprint in some record somewhere

another person praying that their blood doesn't stain, that the person to clean it will not be a loved one

another heart broken with the realization that this may be their last memory

another name got added to the list

another state became a murder zone

another location the last place sunshine will ever feel like meditation
another home became a death trap, a welcome mat, a new hello with a vindictive twist

another lesson of the demons these entryways let loose

another distress call becomes a target practice

another name becomes a chant, becomes a
public masquerade
a political ammunition a foundation for leadership or hype

another stranger coxing tears from the population

another thing stolen from the dead

another name to add when many more are lost like
Dead Sea scrolls
another body discarded without aide

another talent tortured before they can sometimes see
beyond the fear and pray

another soul mistaking death's blue suit as savior, as
protector not reaper

another name the galaxies utter before we do
another public display of carcass and blood splatters artfully
mimicking masterpieces

another shell casting surrounding inkblots webbing walls

another civil servant turned interior decorator using
caution tape as a muse

another tragedy the family tries to make sense of when
we do

another proof that no amount of justice may amount to the souls lost, the souls continued to be lost and hidden

another name they will never say when they claim peaceful marches as hostile protests not knowing it's their reaction that dictates the preservative actions we take, so don't say their names until you have memorized the history of their death, until you can bleed a pain you will not feel, until their wounds become a permanent manifestation in your mouth

until their name slips off your tongue like spittle, not only in the heights of these marches but decades when they have rotted and their stories are overshadowed with new frustrations

say their names until it becomes a testimony of the ones that have no recollection of life or the memories it holds, say their name so you can help the ones that knew them best carry their memories and their story for comfort

Funeral Procession

Once upon a time, I woke with no one around
I saw the hologram of myself push everyone away
And when I died last night, I told myself I would know
who belonged there

Would know the sisterhood of pallbearers that will stand
pushing my bones, my teeth,
my blood back into the parts of their body it can fit as if
securing it for meas if trying to come together to build me
a new citadel, one without the pain they constantly see,
one without the frustration

Without the laughter from church buses
One without the walks home
One without hospital beds and all the wrong cheat codes
for life

I saw my seven angels, and I knew that I had one for every
seal of heaven
See, I got a childhood friend I know will cry to God before
anyone else (B.D.)

A girl I met last year who will write prose and find scientific
reasons for me (J.V.)

Got one who will steal the voice of Whitney because she
only knows grief and praise through music (T.A.)

Got one who introduced me as family even though the same blood didn't run in our veins (R.M.)

Got one who will wish it was her who had the strength and half-heartedly mean it (N.W.)

Got one I call a best friend whose tears will flood this earth if she cannot find a reason why (J.C.)

Got one who would stay silent in grief and walk like she was another one of Job's friends. I call her my traveling soldier (R.G.)

> I pushed my angels away to get more. I think I will hurt
> the same way I
> Told them I never stay long with anyone
> I'm not dependable like that

Now I got
A new one who will recite poetry and write lyrical prose for me and call it her grieving (J.B.)

Got one who will sink beneath the bedsheets of any woman to find out if there is any way a womb can clone something that hasn't lived inside it for 17 years (T.E.)

I still got that childhood friend who will kiss her fears up to God and then question him
and me
and the soul no longer within me and everyone who cares

to listen (B.D.)

Got one who will wonder if my legs ever felt the pain of love before I decided that I was too good for this world (T.S.)

Got one that thinks the books and the Bible and the elderly have all the answers, so she looks into cosmic shit to find answers to what she refuses to understand (A.B.)

I got one who will make sure I'm picture perfect, make sure my flaws are faultless, and I'll always love her for making me laugh at my lowest and if it's ever anything in my power, then I'll support and cheer her on even with my last breath 'cause she introduced me to friends who made all the difference (A.M.)

Got one who holds on so tight to my life that I am scared that she can become my noose if I let her
Scared that if I leave, I will hurt her something inexplicable
And I take my time walking from her
Take my time loving and celebrating her from afar (D.F.)

Take my time checking up because she becomes another daughter
Becomes another staple in my dinner of a disaster
Becomes another sister-friend who cannot call me one (D.F.)

And I am sorry knowing she will never be there when I look into the future

And don't think I forgot the childhood friend who always had my back, made my summers a blessing, being a big Sister handing out lessons, so even when others see her thorns, all I see is the rose beneath the overgrowth (S.R.)

Got another lucky number 17 that I still thank God I met (A.R., M.F., A.T.R., A.T., O.D., B.E., S.H., J.P., S.C., M.R.C., S.F., A.W., S.M., R.W., T.M., C.Y., A.S.)

I'm done with angels, but I love the ones I shuffled along the way
I love the sisterhood and atmosphere they left behind on this unraveling cloth of friendship, support, and love

And every one of them taught me something, and a million more were never mentioned
but still loved 'cause I wouldn't finish if I listed all the qualities they left me with.[17]

---

17 *Bianca Dempster, Jewel Virtue, Tiana Antonio, Racquea Melville, Nadjah-lee Williams, Janel Cunningham, Regina Gayle, Rickay Davis (first written October 19, 2015); Jaynelle Burchelle, Takiyah Edwards, Tanecia Smith, Ashalee Brown, Alyssa Mcleish, Danielle Francis, Shericka Rose, Ashley Ricketts, Morgan Foster, Alexis Taylor-Reid, Abigail Thompson, Omelia Daley, Brehanna Edwards, Shaznae Howe, Julianna Powell, Sejavia Campbell, Monique Rowe-Carter, Shanique Fletcher, Amanda Williams, Sydoni Maitland, Rianna Walters, Taina McKenzie, Charles-Marie Young, and Aaliyah Simpson.*

Eulogy for the unknown

**"And they took council and brought with
them the potter's field to bury strangers in..."**

~ Matthew 27 KJV

I heard that they found a body last night.
It was washed ashore the citarum, piece by a severed
piece and they said it was a girl my age. A girl with no
family, whose black nails housed the blood from the
massacre in her head.[18]
A girl whose fingerprints were smudged in bromine
trioxide and they called her Jane Doe, as if whitewashing
her into something they could look at.

The police said no investigation could be launched
because too many motives danced around the equation.
Besides, nothing on her
was originally her own. Not her nose, her mouth, or her
passing skin tone.

With a lecherous grin, he said he guessed she died before
the inflated breath had time to poison her body.
What a hell of a thing beauty is when it's no longer in the
eyes of the beholder.

And I wondered if they asked themselves, paper or plastic,
as they threw her to the likes of the Thames, because print
today has more bearing than human life. So I wonder if,

when I die, they will discard my memory too? Or frame my words on parchment, sending them to the heavens in the glorious fire of Norse pyres.

And

In my haunted dreams, I heard myself say that I knew that girl. So I took Matthew 27:7 and stood by it.
I couldn't afford the land, but I know the state already has one where there was no respect for the dead if they lived their lives secluded. No obituary for the lost; no pictures or sad words for the people they abandoned to show that even though they were estranged, they still care.

And because I don't believe in deserving that second chance, I wrote the eulogy of someone I know who may be buried in the Potter's Field, and I consummated her by way of last rites before death and cashed in the golden chips under the table so she wouldn't have to lose the voice of pending poets-turned-rappers to the culture of the press who couldn't even slam a door on the taxed words that she didn't patent.

So,
Help me write a eulogy.

Make it a time capsule project for those to come after me.
Let them see that I sing it each night as a lullaby,
keeping one eye open like the greatest watchman of all time, should he pop in like a jack-in-the-box to drape my

shirt like I'm a scatterbrained fool being scolded for ruining the surprise?

I've aligned my lips so many times to give birth to broken syllables, and I see myself hanging upon the words of charred lips singing the opera. As if she isn't dead.
As if she doesn't wonder who found her cold in some ditch, and even then, she doesn't regret a thing.
If given the choice between a hero and a villain, there is no choice at all because villains have more fun than blondes.

you see

This should be a eulogy, but what do you say about someone you don't know?
someone who changes more than a chameleon

Should I stray by saying that I feel bound to tell you that this girl was rather indifferent to intellectual pleasures, since you can't outright call the dead dumb? Should I find fancy phrases and words to say she was a bitch no one loved?

So good riddance to the manipulative prick who only came around when she needed something.
Should I say that I'd rather be slapped silly with hobnailed boots than recommend her memory to the hubbub of people?
Should I require they dismantle her limb from limb and tie her to a square so passersby can stone her with rotten produce until she deteriorates in the belly of pests?

or do I fix my lips to set the whiskey-induced butterflies free from my tongue as I appease the gods for having good dharma?
and no drama, and the body found was mine.
but it wasn't in the papers.

My face was structured, never to be remembered. I still kick in bed, saying that's not me because if I paid for my death then I can orchestrate for it never to be found.

CHAPTER IV
Bildungsroman or something like that

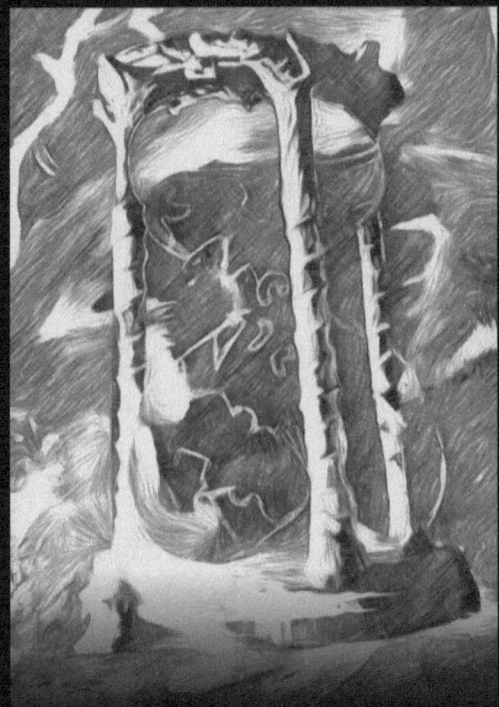

Wendell Berry once said that the past is our definition.
We may strive with good reason to escape it, or to escape what
is bad in it. But we will escape it only by adding something
better to it.

My bars be like healing[19]

Be like lost pirate treasures and Columbus' pillaging and
conquering.
Like Black folks marching through the slickness of the blood
of the Nile
Be painful, like first sons dying.
My bars be thick with morals like a fisherman's compass.
Have hooks to keep you interested in my story line, not just
the one that comes from the pits of my thighs.
My bars be sour like lime,

Bars got truth and bitterness flowing from Ahab's vines.
Hold up, my bars sound historical and Biblical, but they
got electric clips and filed off serial numbers with Wyatt
Earp's blessings.

Yes, my bars played Double Dutch in playgrounds while
hustling, where Nipsey never did.
And
My bars be like assassins to the saints of the church.
Be like spilling diluted truth into robes of gold.
Bars be like throbbing clits when you inhale captivating
scents.
Bars be like emptying the bitter red wine of his side to mix
Canaan's river of milk and honey.
Bars be like piranhas strangling men with my feet.

See my bars
My bars are seductive, like sirens stealing the souls of men.

Bars got men choking and drowning in my God-given waters.
Got women lapping like dogs at the doors of my womb because my bars are smooth enough to pull both.
My bars got the rhythm of my mind's hips dancing in Spanish clubs, saying *"Te amo mas que baby."*

My bars be lyrically inclined like she was on the come up with Lady London,
spits like she majored with Lady Lava
educated like Spice

My bars fluent in her flow like Joyner Lucas
My bars be rich in fluidity
And my bars,
My bars stop on railway tracks to save the depressed and suicidal who, like the wife of Lot, have seen quicksand swallow the brimstones of Sodom and Gomorrah.

And you want to tell me that your bars fought with Putin, but my bars are like Ezekiel resurrecting
dried bones.
So don't define me by your bars, because your bars aren't my bars.
My bars be like serpents sliding around your girls' necks, twisting like childhood swings.
Bars got her moaning and out of breath, as if pleasure is all new to her.

yes

My bars are proof that you haven't earned your manhood yet.
My bars resemble the FBI's most wanted list.
See my bars; find you dead or alive.
My bars are shanks for prison fights because Folsom isn't the only one with blues.
My bars are unruly like a girl throwing knives; these guns don't phase me because I got bars like Shakespearean tragedies.

My bars be hidden gardens inducing herbs unknown
to men
My bars be country and prose
Be all church and dancehall
Be cowgirls and ferry rides
Tennis and cricket, my bars diversified,
got talent like Viola and Taraji
Fists like Muhammed Ali and Jon Jones
My bars rupture a drowning in her vocals just to freestyle
like Alia Atkinson
My bars be seductive too, borrow sorrow and sexiness to
give and take from paramours
got men and women tangled in the nectar of my tongue,
has them dueling for the promises of life God made
way back when

My bars got them to fake amnesia and forget themselves in the home of my art.

See my bars.

My bars launched the ships Helen's face couldn't
and my bars ate the carcass of a lion like Samson.

My bars spat on Golgotha and taught the Corinthians what
the gospel means.
because my bars know there is only one God, and he's not
unknown.
So let my bars be your oracle for prophecies and peace.

because

My bars haven't even begun to get good yet.

The first time I couldn't write

It felt like an eviction, so I no longer call my body a home, for without words, it is more tombstone church than headrest.
The first time I couldn't write, I felt like I was drowning in gasoline and set on fire, so I learned to swim
pre-pugilistic attitude
The first time I couldn't write,
I physically felt the words playing hopscotch over my imagination, and I asked a child to teach me her innocence.

The first time I couldn't write
I tried to remember the last time my tongue swirled in the bakery of poetry to finger gunpowder,
and like the wanderer I am, I began to wonder if I had used metaphors of cinnamon to kill a mockingbird instead of a blue jay, and I thought maybe this was punishment for that.

The first time I couldn't write, I didn't speak to God for months.
I didn't want him to realize my shame in squandering a gift, that I could never Houdini into a talent,
so I pushed my accolades before me like I was Israel ebbing the anger of Esau.
And
I didn't cry either, but I became an alchemist, searching for the meaning behind a vibrating heart with no words to comfort it.
So when the vivacious tones of this body refused me a home, I wondered if I could use thaumaturgy to make a temporary

dwelling where no one would put me out.
Then I wondered what would happen if I woke up and couldn't write. How many nights would I sleep in the cold while time choked the congested rhymes out of me?

How many times will I look society in the eyes as they tell me I will never make it doing art?

And I think back on the kind of prestidigitation that will make them believe that I can create any art form when I whisper through the window of trauma.

So call me fantasizer,
Call me witless call me actress, but never forget
to call me writer,
For I am everything and nothing when I escort the truth to straddle what's left of the dopamine in the brain,
because without words I am left homeless, and sometimes all I am is homeless because there are days I cannot write.

There is a funny thing that happens whenever I get nervous

I roll my tongue into a 4 leaf clover and rename it good luck before taking my greatest fears to God in prayer as if this mendelian inheritance was his way of telling me I could be rare, could be special.

I spin the wheel of fortune on the finger made for marriage. I think that the scorching heat as my skin expands over the band is sentimental enough not to give into the fire crashing against the waves, which a good pure child of God should not think of, and I am caught holding onto bars that brand themselves onto me. This reminds me that anything great is worth the wait.

When I get nervous, I am caught kidnapping my breath and refusing to let it go, even after the ransom is paid.

I am caught holding my beating heart and pinning caution lines around it, like it's a bloody crime scene made for forensic experts.

When I get nervous I bite my fingernails and hope that it is enough nutrition for the abatement of fear. I hope that it is enough last meal to fill the rumbling barrels of my stomach. When I get nervous, I cough up the messages pulled from my scalp and litter them between corn stalks barefoot and howling.

When I get nervous, my lungs drown themselves in mucus, daring my body to kill me to extinguish the charcoal fumes that are lost within. When I get nervous, I tap my feet and sigh the rhythms of compositions Mozart have never heard of.

When I get nervous, I stare into space for hours, refusing to move should the walls grow feet and walk away.

When I get nervous, I press my index and middle fingers together and press lightly to remind myself that if you look hard enough you can find a pulse in a suicidal woman.

When I get nervous,I bite at the flesh within my mouth to see what blood tastes like or to smell how death would feel if it were messy enough to leave crimson dust patterns.

When I get nervous, I am able to count every teardrop, announce every banner of war, lose my white flag of surrender, and play dead.

When I get nervous , I write poems like these that make no sense, that ache to be burned, that shout back from the microphone of God that they are unworthy enough to be heard, and the funny thing about when I get nervous is that I get nervous a lot.

My grandmother's Treasures

My grandmother never stuck around to meet me, but I heard that she passed her face to me in her last will and testament, as if laying claim to a prize she would have treasured had not death loggered her from us. I've walked her hometown, where people still see me with a head-tie and a scowl, and you would think that my age was my saving grace, but these people, well, they claim that it's my skin tone. You see, the woman whose face I inherited had a skin the shade of ebony roasted in olives. Her demeanor, unlike mine, was graceful, and I heard that she still walks behind me. In each step I take, she has armies guarding my way should I fall prey to the darkness of the land. I never met this kin of mine whose church sisters sang her praises like they were more magnificent than the pyramids of King Tut. I never met this kin whose hands could spin fortunes from nothing to feed more than 10 hungry mouths. Who valued education and food like they were the keys to living right. I never met the woman whose hustle never stopped her fashion sense. Whose goal was to give her kids all she never got, but I know that someday I will make her proud for choosing to continue her legacy with me. I'll make her proud for lamenting albums and antiques and storing them in the barracks of her home so that I may someday creep beneath the earth just to preserve the mildewed history that is my family from losing sight of what is most important, and that is and always will be forgiveness and unity.

Masterpiece

If I were a painting,
I'd have the mysteries of the *Mona Lisa* thinking of 365 ways
to die with the craze of the *Starry Night* clouding my eyes.
I'll be laying my head on the guillotine for Artemisia to
capture the moment that *Judith slays Holofernes*. I bet he
doesn't drink in hell.
I'll be the *Girl with a Pearl Earring*, clutching *The Birth
of Venus* in my hands and making sure they know that I
can still be an incorruptible lady. But never really ladylike.
Serenading men and women with *The Kiss*, should they ever
stare long enough into my geometry of PDA.

If I were a painting,
I'd be *The Night Watch*, no Game of Thrones plot My Walther
pistol perfectly balanced on trench saps. Praying in my
heart that back home, *The Whistler's Mother* doesn't eat
dinner with the last woman who raised me.
Because war, they say, came with a few design flaws that
won't ever go away.
And I hope she doesn't fear white lightning as if they were
brass shell casings. I hope she doesn't draw the curtains
and listen to the church bell tolling.
But who is to say she didn't already comfort herself and
turn the lights out, thinking I wouldn't ever come home?

If I were a painting,
I'd be *The Guernica* playing hangman with memories that
leave me surgically amputating my hippocampus.

And looking for a portal to reverse the past in my future, should I suffer tragedies from the battlegrounds I didn't clear and find peace with white walkers buried beyond the wall without forgiveness, a pyre be damned. But I still hope Floki made it to Valhalla.

That he saw Ordin and told him I don't really follow tradition, so I had to end him before he killed my vision.

If I were a painting,
I'd be *The American Gothic* wearing camouflaged breeches to shovel manure in Wellington boots because when I faced my *Great Depression*, I watched livestock play quidditch and listened to rainfall on crops.

I promise that is the simplest life can ever get, and I will always miss that. But don't be mistaken.

I came from the *Bathers at Asnières* and ended up on a Sunday afternoon on the *Island of La Grande Jatte*, so I'm not too bougie, because no matter where you go you have to keep an open mind.

If I were a painting,
I'd be *The Last Supper*, telling my organs that surely one of you will betray me, as I wipe my monocle to see them squirm and slosh in their liquids, sulking like innocent schoolgirls trying to hide nefarious plots. And my lungs keep saying not me, but like Peter, she will never have my back. My heart still takes lessons from doubting Thomas, and my brain sings suicidal riddles like she's Judas Iscariot. I wish I could tell them that one would stand up, but my kidneys fail to the berceuse of sorrows like a drowsy James

and John.

If I were a painting,
I'd be as insignificant as the mirrored aristocrats in *Las Meninas*. A background shadow listening in to the gossipy lady's maid about the things they see and hear in the courtyard, I'd be having the time of my life. But still, as swift as *The Fox*, and I know I'd be as confused as the painting itself.

If I were a painting,
I'd be the *Bal Du Moulin De La Galette*, using alcohol as a temporary salve for numb wounds.
I'd take to the limelight and strike a few bar fights, and let it be known that in that moment I'll tell you that I know how to hold my liquor. I won't say sike unless you can recall the trigger events of five wars. I think you'll find out on your own that I can't drink half a glass, but I take Wray and his nephew like I'm a desert camel taking water.

If I were a painting,
I'd be *The Persistence of Memory*, knowing that in the end all I have are the moments and sometimes they don't really seem to matter that much when I don't have a backup drive for this program of mine. And I don't think it's normal that it's not long-term or short-term. It just dries up the minute I leave it out of sight.

So I live vicariously in *The School of Athens* through my subconscious to prove Plato's theory that reality isn't real;

it's the thinking that's important, and to many, that's seen as boring, so they tend to watch the red-tail lights of youth flutter by knowing that they lived to work and dream, but what does it matter if it all fails in the end?

If I were a painting,
It would be those few seconds in the night when everything goes silent, drinking lemon tea at the *Isolated Café Terrace* at night watching *White Swans* illuminated by the dancing of the moonlight as I close my eyes, hoping I'm not closer to the ground than I originally thought.
I'd want to take a flight in the night like the *Sleeping Gypsy* because the Impression of Sunrise is always so watered down.
I'm *The Wanderer* above the sea of fog blanketed in controversy, pining away at the long arm of the law that fails society.

If I were a painting,
I'd be the *Les Demoiselles D'Avignon*, for my name too annoys me, but I'd unravel my truths of idealism and convention because people fear what they don't understand, and if I speak in riddles like a pixie, they can't thwart the escape plans all women must make to survive.

So I'll use the pen as my sword, and if it's as mighty as they say then you'll listen closely to twenty-one paintings of complication and mystery that are cultured just the same. I have twenty-one possibilities and far more dreams, but I've never felt so incomplete.

It turns out that I've always been a painting.

Sprawled white on canvas with no design or scrawl passed my indentation,
For only then will I have a chance to dream of my realities.

Born to die; voice of the undead

I don't remember how I was born.
How the half-baked remnants of cackling fire in my mother's
uterus shoved me forward to ride the wings of angels

I guess Aphrodite saw fit to give life to a baby of Erebus, but
my mother told me that I somehow clung to the phaeton
of destruction despite the fighting she gave to live and give
life. And I survived.

They called me a miracle baby, said the world would strike,
but I had the willpower of Thor.
And Zeus, well, he was my guide through the hollow waters
of the Lethe between my mother's core.

And when I started talking, I thought I was learning to
express myself. Promised to always speak my mind, and at
first there was no man left behind when the playground of
my tongue swung back in its saddle and struck.
They said I played with words like an arsonist played with
fire.
A little red devil swinging on the front steps, playing Ring
Around the Rosey because life was a bed of roses, and
pitchforks tossed my body round and round, sandwiching
me in the bliss of the moment.

But did you know I was ten when I learned to keep my
mouth shut? When I finally knew this world wasn't fair and
kept my eyes spinning in the cracked sockets of the earth's

skull, the truth introduced me to
So I clammed up and said change was inevitable.
Did you know that sometimes I feel like going insane?
And I wondered if this was the first step in realizing you
needed help. My doctor said I was fine.
that my doubling caused me to live this dystopia in my own
utopia, so somehow I couldn't see behind the blinds I've
caged myself in. I stayed awake for 20 hours a day because
I knew I couldn't stop thinking. I guess I suffered from
mnemophobia.

She prescribed forgiveness.

Believe it or not, I didn't take the time to forgive, but I built
my own personality.
This is who I wanted to be, and now I can't shut up.
Intropin in the tracks of my nuclei running faster than the
Rio Cobre. I used to hold onto me as a miracle baby, but I
forgot for a minute that I'm not supposed to be alive. And
maybe that's the reason why I'm not afraid to die because
I've been there before. Have stared between the ledgers
wishing a coin would land my way for once padding me in
options that may finally decapitate the zombified memories
I've laid to rest.

Fetal demise

I don't know who the girl in the mirror is anymore.
But I toe-tagged the one with the heartbeat from her
clitoris, should sorrows blossom into success and I watched
as they Mayflowered through the iceberg to push the Bible
through my jugular and talk about Holy Ghost death.
So, I've been chewing iron blocks of euthanasia hoping its
mercy is better virtue than suicide.

Now should I be asked to weld the cavity in the ark of my
metra, I will tell them that
These twisted roads have somehow adulterated the glorified
truth. That no one said that the heart could be lost in me.
Just that feticide was not an option to save the life of the
mother. The knots in my stomach meant it was time I
searched through mountains of dirty dishes to find his rib
and hand it back to him. because I was no longer worthy
of the title of woman.

of mother

Now the girl in the mirror keeps watch without lamps.
Hiding under fiery bushels, should someone remind her?
that what she did was an unbridled sin?
But this girl has been brought to the mosque to watch the
fruit depart from her loins.
Now she's screaming at God that He doesn't know her
anymore.
That his word has left the lips of ophidians to define her

And maybe somewhere under his hap
She can find solace in the irregular tempo of her pelvis. And
dance on shattered glass bottles.
For she is forgiven of the zygote that never came for
Hecatomb. They said that in her thirst for redemption
She threw the baby out with the bath water.
Saw the Titanic sink with her faith and asked God
To bless the genius grains of dirt she will meet in
heaven,should he keep the tainted ashes from raining upon
her bare fig tree
She swears, she's learning what emotion is.

So,
In each tempest, she is victorious, for her gun lies within
the pit of her Bible. Yet, she is still crying through the
sarcophagus in her jaw that
She is woman.
And should they not see her?
She'll throw the stones lodged within her fists.
And make them know that the name he wrote in the sand
is hers. In plundering the desolate coastlines of herself, she
has begat the girl in the mirror. And she is the vindication
of the woman with the quiver in her Eden.

The difference between a stripper and a poet may just be the very same

Like a Jehovah Witness I too have spent life blindly handing out love like they were church pamphlets. Believing that in every arm that stretched forth itself it would learn to find home or at least boomerang back to every body caught on top of mine in the moonlight, or to every hopeless romantic throwing dollar bills and snaps at the sight of thong and ass showing no regard for face or voice.

So, I became a poet in the hopes that words would swim through the canal of my vocals, enchanting enough to be a nectar sweeter than eggs scrambling their way out of endorphins dollar bills triggered.

I said I became a poet with the belief that vivacious words would be a philosophy sweating from the benign grind of my tongue so I practiced my game face and stood at damp ground asking the woman sharing my face to see me through this gift of mine. This gift whose roar still have a powerful pull. Wished the blush in its pink is spilled; bleeding petals and dominating elevation that possesses women and men to compete for my attention and this risk I take may just end my life.

May just be the reels of venereal disease pivoting a sinking ship of heroines who spend their days in the aroma of strangers' bed, how different is a poet spending nights on stage collecting snaps while watching the climax of brains with ego pressed upward like their mouth not just their p***y is some sort of dying majik too?

And I realize that there is no difference between being a stripper or a poet because they still please an audience dependent on seeing them at their most vulnerable. Still issue flows that fuel adrenaline and dopamine to make them feel good inside to take some sort of edge or pain away.

The difference between poets and a stripper is that poets, juggle words and demons with the lubricant of their tongue instead of barely jiggling asses and tits and issue them kisses from their pole of a microphone, so when they face new demons before your eyes, I wonder if they ever get tired of loving the dream instead of the act? If the performance ever lost its attachment to the applause, would they consider zipping up the mess they made of their own definition of poets?

I think all poets are strippers, or all strippers are poets with their words flowing from another set of tools and lips, and ain't it great to be in league with women as brave as this? Ain't it great to see how fluid art truly is?

They say when you get a gift

The cardinal rule is that of No Takebacksee, No Tradeoffs, and that applies to all gifts from God but death and the natural order of things that shouldn't be natural, that shouldn't happen so often, that we no longer bat an eyelash at.

That trading the gift of knowledge for eternal life ain't living. Ain't following the order of things worth it, when it gives you jobs, gives you hope.

A thorn on the blossom of roses made to confuse us, and this gift I walk in with, cupped towards my stomach, I usher back to God for it has sold me lies that sacrifice and broken records in the mind were all worth survival.

Was all worth waterboarding fears in Lake Erie.

All worth looped seasons named by ghosts.

That this gift was all halal blessing and curse tied into origami shapes and stuffed down my throat. Was all boombox for the ideologies of one of God's strongest. All music and rhyme for audiences with a half empty appetite for pain, for struggle, for a new definition and outlook on people they have unabashedly damaged and wrongfully convicted victims acquitted on my voice only. On my words, on my tense and grammar and ain't Eve right for eating the fruit but ain't Adam wrong for not picking from life too?

And this gift I would trade in any day for a taste of life past 120, or better yet, past Methuselah's age.

The ingredients of my tears

I once caught myself in conversation with the moon. She said numbness and cold were all she knew.

But she wouldn't dare teach me to languish bitterness upon my tongue. She'd learned long ago to love from afar.

so those within the darkness may never see the dim faults in her stars. And, she stayed away from her lover for years.

She said that the ones we never fear are those that hold hilts, hiding blades. So, I shouted that my tongue was sharp! She chuckled and said the ingredients of my tears are those who claimed to mend me by dislodging bones.

The ingredients of my tears are girls who cry within my 12 hours of reign for help; they never get . The ingredients of my tears are unanswered prayers my lips have never uttered.

The ingredients of my tears are streets outlined with bodies that death has greedily devoured.

The ingredients of my tears are lined within the myriads of destruction this world has yet to see.

You cannot be more upset than me,

My tears have meaning, and they've been here for years.

Smoke filled my lungs, and I blew it towards her.
as she sipped from a high ball glass, her eyes low, heart
dismayed
I said my tears may have no meaning.
but they come from somewhere too.
with ingredients besmirched beneath collapsing lungs
I've learned to lay awake numerous nights attempting to
dig up memories, tombs, and
bones.
Wishing someone had warned me not to bury daggers in
gold
I suppose I should learn to love scars.
because I've never had life as hard as you, who sit so high
and never once get involved.

Instead, I've walked this flat plain for a little bit too long.
stuffed silence into haunting cracks
and found loopholes in games lost to love.
The scars I've borne know no ghost,
no home.
no, me
Just that they too need to be loved.

Her cold eyes ignited like a raging fire burnt within.

She said I never said numbness was never feeling hurt.
Or joy, or both. just that it's the only word you can hold that
will never let you down.
but I wouldn't let her finish.
for the ingredients of my tears were not even started.

It's not the beginning that holds you hostage, but the escaping that brings you there again, almost like a broken record. causing life to sss..st...stutter.
Or a recurring nightmare making sure your hell may never end.

It's like having a heart of gold that's as light as a feather. flutters as paper and burns like wood.

It's being the wind but having no air.

It's a museum with no history.

A tomb without a ghost

Rain without lightning, wind, water or clouds

It's realizing how dangerous you are.
So, you just stay away.

The ingredients in my tears are why I keep them all inside.
And in all my wrongs,
I've never been torn so far apart.
Infected explanations fluttering through my thoughts,
what to make of them,
I may never understand.
And if like her you believe that the ingredients of my tears shouldn't matter, because it's no more than people have,

here's an empty list.
Keep it as a souvenir so someday you too may remember
that I don't have an answer for arteries overflowing,
and maybe one day my ocular fluids won't be such a
mystery, and you'll have the ingredients you need to see
them fall.

But for now, the only ingredient in my tears is me.
She had left before I had finished speaking. Camouflaged
within the clouds like a beauty queen going back to her king.

Leaving sandpaper scratching at the door of my throat as
a streak raced to the floor.
Turns out that the ingredient of my tears may be me.

But that day I realized it's also those who left me to believe; I
was never a reason to stay. And I believe the greatest lesson
that she taught me was that It's both a blessing and a curse.
Sometimes abandonment does not create tears. But joy
instead.

Miscarriage of hope

I've relapse, laced my fractured thoughts with lead
And now I understand what they meant when they said
that I must give birth to healing.
but after having my cervix dilate to empty my fetus
I gag on the placenta having shoveled a part of survival in
my body
See, I do not know how to give life to anything, have
barricaded the parts of me feminine enough to carry or
push something full term
So if I must give birth to healing my prayers have changed
see, I now pray for rain.
Now pray to remove the training wheels from my heart
before my mouth is fully potty-trained to follow its
instructions. And not those of my brain.

For once, I want the voice that sounds like me to scare
demons instead of welcoming them.
To give home to the piranhas of purity
I want to live long enough to be agile in flight, like the bats
in my womb.
Yes, I've relapsed, but I promise I'm not a junkie.
If manifestation begets reality then I will spit the same lies
they do until I am strong enough to stop when these pills
want me to.
See, their love still crawls beneath spaces not worthy of me.
Maybe I feel trapped outside the box of societal standards
and I want to be included and alive.
I want to have pride in who I am, but I also want to be alone

and secluded.

I guess I should tell you now rather than later.

I've been to the crack house.

Have seen how they hold onto souls and corrupt the mind, and I still drank the waters of Golgotha.

I went looking for the oracle of Delphi in the mouths of self-assessed therapists.

And I was too focused on finding the hole in my pill bottle that I didn't acknowledge the fire I've been extinguishing for so long. And I relapsed.

Baby this is healing so I don't need that pity in your eye or for you to psychoanalyze me.

Instead, can you kiss me one last time?

And make me feel as if your fingertips had magic that only I knew the cords to.

Like the caress of your tears and a gentle bite on my skin are diamonds, So Baby, I've healed, and I'm starting to love. But somehow,

I think I've deprived myself of feeding you my body without knowing me. But this

This is not a goodbye or blame game. I'll see you soon.

Until then, can you hold the strings that guide me in the shrine of your arms? This healing I'll bring full term this time around, not for you, but so that I can prove that God has somehow not forsaken me. And in purging my Canaan, he's given me the greatest jewel of faith.

Halfway to heaven

you may think it's crazy when I tell you I have seen my death.
and remember the day I almost died.
I still remember my head lolling side by side and voices so
far off asking me to stay with them.
I was halfway to heaven when I realized I wasn't ready. So,
I saw myself playing Jenga to save time.
stacked my bones on each other.
pecked at the pieces that weren't blameless and perfect
I spent the minutes in flight.
concealing blemishes that seemed to boomerang back but
I needed to hide who I had sculpted me to be.
So, I screamed checkmate to the bingo masters. so they
wouldn't see beyond my mask.
Did I tell you I was fond of games? or that I was afraid of
losing?
So, I stuck to my grounding and played it safe. I told him I
had devoured his word and won. but as I watched my soul
float in the Nile
I realized denial was the Ganges of Thames in my quarters.
And as lightning struck and the curtain split,
I tried sneaking past the mafia host of Talibans in my home.
that were cloned as flesh of my flesh
Blood of my blood
I told him I didn't know they were there in the first place
He probably knew I was lying by the way I hid my face like
Adam.
I must have been Adam, knowing his word.
but tempted by the succubus in me to deny I ever heard

it. yes,
I've been in the crusades but haven't yet placed chips on
the silver linings of alters.
I thought I did him a favor, and he owed me a favor.`

And if I cashed it in, I would walk freely through his
chambers. No need for stones to stand as me
See, if it weren't for his blood on my hands, I may still walk
Damascus. Now I'm positive life was worth living.
And halfway to heaven, Selene showed me the staircase to
the comatose girl in church.
whose glazed eyes seemed so lonely, and I knew I couldn't
go.
couldn't leave until her comforter had come, and she was
positive about her destination.
So, I turned back and came to earth.
washed her soiled robes and
I cleansed myself of sins untold.
And I watched him write my name in that book he held.
So, forgive me if the next time my life flashes before me, I
won't hold my breath. because I know now that maybe then
I won't get the chance to change my tracks.
I was halfway to heaven. and somehow, I realized it was a
lesson, not a dream
I was halfway to death, and he was willing to tell me to
prepare myself.
Now, should I ever be kidnapped by Thanatos?

I won't be surprised to see his face.

Charmed

I wish I could say that I'm immortal or that I believe in infinity. The truth is, I don't believe in the supernatural.
But I do believe there are things we can't explain in this world of changing times. And I fear to think of the things we've unknowingly dabbled in. See, I once believed that poets were the real magicians. the superior witches who escaped the trial of the Basque that in burning our communes, We scattered like the men building the tower of Babble, but Now, I have proof that there is a David wielding mics in every tribunal circle.

And I remember the first time I charmed my pen and thought that only a few rappers knew this word play.
that the psalms of my vocals could shake any mountain
But the surprise on their faces must have been shared by society before the power of enlightened words caused the fear-fueled massacre.
and I wonder,
How long will they be captivated by my voice before they shout to burn the witch, whose words juggled the keys of life and death? So, I've used vocabulary infused in Valerian steel to tiptoe around their intellect.

While aiming my smoking 25 at every Black site and making sure I wasn't seen as a threat, I've lost myself in trying to please them. now, hear me scream bloody hell at rumors of witch hunts,
While I sit, flossing chauvinistic words from the lips of men

just to recycle them
Watch me create new futures by forever playing cricket
with their balls. So I won't be prey to the same tired lines
women have coddled in hopes of love, and I tell them that
I have adopted the fear of deference should they not hear
me without threats of prosecution.

And I want to think that I do it all just to show that the
patriarchy is dead. And art is not a curse but a blessing.
and I'm not willing to grieve it just yet.
there is no story I can tell that I won't stand behind. because
words have always danced for me, like I'm dyslexic.
like I've earned my place in their shadows to hide this urn
where crusaders won't ever find me, No pun is intended.

He said, "Multiply your talents"
but I've buried them because I'm not ready to find the
secrets of the dead. Look at me.
I'm just a woman who feels the need to play with words.
too polite to say what I mean. So, I've employed metaphors
to slave for me, hoping that those who hear them can't
decipher the cryptogram. if they don't have the key
But
If I'm a witch, how come
I haven't learned how to wield my wand to shift reality.
And if you ever find that out, can you help me tell non-
believers to Take my hand and lead me to the Pharisees?
so Jehovah can witness me spend sunrise to sunset, missing
the Sabbath to spill the ink he gave me. Let them burn me
at the stake with a mic down my throat.

I'm the masterpiece of Aristotle.
a necromancer, resurrecting dead tongues. and hooking hookers on my palmistry like Jesus did. Isn't language a funny thing?

Truth be told, I used to fear the power I held.
Now I embrace it and the challenges ahead, so if you must burn me, Burn me with a story in the cinerarium of my throat.
Adopt it into your home and tell it to the world.
But remember, the thing that won't ever die on any cross is the power of my words.
I don't have to believe it, but I think this is what immortality is: the envied power of three: vocabulary, ink, and parchment.

Facts about me

At times, I wonder if you ever wonder who the girl behind the screen is, and I tried to find her for you? So I thought of writing down some facts about myself.

That was six months ago, and since then, the paper in me has kept staring back, waiting impatiently for a scar on its face as proof that it survived the worst of earthquakes hurled from the pit of my esophagus, as if I had the guts to simply slap an identity onto her without first knowing what side to show to people I barely know.

But I think I finally got it, so like always, I'll trade joint aches for the dull parts of me that seem so fun to me.
Trade hanging from monkey bars to learn the secrets removed from the grout of life.

Ask me to introduce myself, and I'll whisper.
Hi there, I'm 18 years old, and for as long as I can remember, I've always believed that God should be thanked, not begged. But when I see sunsets and rainbows, I'm left begging for my anger to be abated because I get queasy just thinking about how creation has become a mockery to people whose chalk outlines are fugitives.

So in those moments, I tear my faith from my heels to hide beneath my bed from God because, in those moments, I think his spilled body and blood represented ours.

My favorite colors are gray and white, and I binge drink and smoke so that I can feel something that's not the lightning from the cloud above my head. I love Shakespearean tragedies, and my favorite opera is Queen of the Night. Because a side of me refuses the knives I hear should have killed me, I tend to make jokes about depression because my panic episodes don't give way to externalizing my psychotic breaks.

I love erasers because, like a kindergartener, I've adapted the method of erasing my mistakes as if they weren't the parts of me that I felt threatened by.
Like many Black men, my favorite meal is not on the budget of death row, but I know that if I die, I'd want to eat jerk pork because it's the only savory dish that can bring me joy in pain stitched timelines

I don't want to be buried in satin.
I want to be cremated so as to hide the words that were once embroidered into the calico of my skin and served as a memo to my brain because sometimes I get amnesia from swallowing so much of the world and I need to remember who I am.

I have no reaction to feeling numb, and I can't keep explaining how it is not like sadness, emptiness, or anything else.

I hate that every time I write, I kidnap Biblical allusions to become somewhat of a signature.
Because every time I think of stepping outside into the

world for a better reference, I remember that the weapon in me is jammed. So I keep my head down because everyone else walks with their safety off.

I suck at confrontation and expressing myself, so I've taken the backseat to my life and shoplifted survival modes by punching holes into my pillar as if beauty needed help from miniature stainless steel pins and IV lines stealing blood to keep you thin inside.

I love hurricanes and thunderstorms because they help me focus on the truth that there's a possibility that I won't wake up in the morning, and I love the gamble of making plans I may not keep. I hate walking in the rain or after it because it washes the streets raw for new sin.

My favorite weather is the coldest, and my favorite season is the changing of autumn, where I can watch the withering of life before its rebirth and be okay knowing that it's a beautiful thing, this thing called death.

I know I failed to introduce myself, and you probably have more questions than answers, but the way my brain works is funny, dark, and weird, and I hate staying in here too.

I do not like Halloween or horror movies,

but I like the sorcery of gothic tales.
I like to give body to my haunting and let her walk these
pews searching for an incline of fear to her next target. And
in respect of the season, I came prepared to sink my teeth
into a horror tale for you.
I dug up my own mummy and sat her here as the scariest
thing I have ever lived through spews from her lips as
decoration for truly awful ones I do not yet own.

I do this with spirits racing in me, for I cannot face her
memory sober. And my mummy starts her tale by saying
"Whoever said all girls look for their father in a man before
looking for compatibility "lied.

Fun fact I do not look for men at all or any relationship for
that matter I do not wish for marriage so that I can embrace
the white noise that sees my father crawl from the pores of
my veins. I'm too afraid that his touch will come hawking
up in each whisper of a touch

That his voice will Eve's Bayou itself into our home, and I ask
the witch to specter another memory worth remembering,
and she tells me I am cursed she tells me that the wax coffin
has my hairs in it, and my hairs are also his gene that my
power is not of sight but of a black widow's, and I embrace
that knowledge. Become a cactus sprouting cattail spikes to
lay the foundation for healing, thinking that I could rewrite
a generation of curses without facing them first. And I learnt

to cut him from my veins.

The first time his memory transitioned from one personality to another, I cried, said stop, threw a "no" that uno reversed itself as a synonym for "f**k you" watched him counterintelligence this into a trick, like my mind ain't smart enough to know this ain't protection.

And that was the first time I knew this man for who he was—the day I replaced his memory with one I could not name. This was the first time I had an asthma attack that no one could cure. It was the first time a disembodied arm took hold of my lungs and squeezed so tight that I could not remember what it felt like to breathe properly before this. I didn't know how dying felt until my limbs spilled themselves to cover my nakedness, until I watched bathroom doors turn curtains so anyone could enter, and ain't it funny how he always searched for what God placed in me?

If I could write all my memories of my father, you would never be able to sleep past the haunting that will climb its way into you. And this poem is not another daddy's girl lesson, it is one saying her daddy was no blessing. Permanent missing fixture ruining her outlook on everything

It is not another lady looking for her father in a man
Is one telling you that not all women do

Is one saying that not all little girls have high hopes for relationships

This ain't a list for girls comforting themselves saying they will never go back there or that they aren't worthy enough of anything good like they ain't still packing and unpacking that baggage all their life and the day he told them I fought him, he did not tell them what he did and the last time he touched me, I did what I have thought about doing the first time sprouted knife blades beneath my tongue so sharp I cut the legs from under him just by opening my mouth and letting loose all the dirty laundry he hid beneath his power and my fear and my silence.

That day, I learned survival.
That day, I learned how golden silence really isn't.

And no matter how long I spend cutting his blood from my veins, I realized he will still be a part of me. I will still hate that I am a part of him. And that is the first time I become so afraid of history, the reason I cannot get too attached for fear this resurrects itself into the home I one day build or becomes a shadow echoing its call of death in my children's children's home.

The art of a boxed up unpacked life

When I first moved from the complacency of the past and the clutter of realism, I never knew that what I didn't box would follow me into the new world.

Until
I found myself unpacking the last box of my father's, took it to the curb, and tore the fragile stickers off.

and waited in vain for the December cold air to cut through plexiglass secured by bubble-wrapped foam boards that I couldn't bring myself to recycle with my new decor.

but
Frostbites failed to chisel themselves into blood vessels like streptococci on skin. So I took a cab back and called home. held the box up to my head, placed my ear on the symbols of déjà vu, and threw my childhood out the window. Hoping that someone could sell what could be salvaged from varying years.

When tears still washed the fingerprints from panel glasses that no longer held them hostage,
And it's funny how I love the villains in the stories but hate the monsters in reality because they are never quite the same when they pop up from the libraries inside of crèches.

And I hear them say,
"Damn, here she goes again, still writing about old shit that

she should have been too young to remember."

So I broke the mold that made me, but I didn't throw the clay away. I guess I thought if I found peace in art, I could sculpt memories I'd be fond of. But I keep crushing on these men who come too close to me because I can't protect them from my ideologies of security when all I know is a gallow of love twisted around my neck and I won't feel too good forcing them to follow me behind trains that don't know when to stop on command.

Yet Simon says I'm acting like I'm still on slave ships.
giving my power to the authority that failed me before living for myself, and I do it too well.
Simon says I replaced his authority with my own because I was groomed for disappointment too young.
Now Simon says he spies something in the sky, and I only see chalk lines and blood-filled casting shells in the simplicity of Nimbostratus clouds. And
My therapist says I'm getting better at identifying intangible ghost objects in inkblots, but she still doesn't know that the first time I saw trauma, it was from the ground up.

I remember staring into headlights that crashed into me like roadkill, and I tried to remember how directing the traffic of U-Hauls and garbage trucks from my driveway could lead to this.

So this time, when I moved out of my head, I boxed the last piece of my father up.

and I'm still finding new roots and holding on to weeds because I'm scared of the unknown and what forgiving him will eventually mean.

I boxed the last of my father up and said to the world, "I'm ready" because I survived what should have killed me. So come do your worst; I'll be here waiting.

Right here, where I murdered the silence of the girl inside me.

Identity crisis

I wasn't a boy named Sue, but I too grew up handing over inkblots of original documents that reflected alphabets quilted into horrid words. Forcing me to gnash my teeth as I inscribed its spelling on binding elements of formal settings, as if I was proud of hoisting ancient relics of horror for all to see.

somehow they saw Benjamin button and his sagging flesh instead of a baby still coated and slippery in the spilling of maternal blood and chose to scare the youth with borrowed issues from almanacs as if modernization was lost upon them.

In their defense, the urban dictionary has said that at first glance, they saw me as noble, as if I should embrace the fact that I am not just a backwashed version of European syllables, but now its meaning proves that I am also chained to the tears of my kinsfolk because I was never rewarded with epithets that slid off the tongue. In their opening statements, I was told to love it because it was common and easy to pronounce. And
I think that they have misguided themselves into thinking that making it easy for others made it right, and so they are still blinded to the torture that I endured in my formative years.

I can't remember who handed it off, but I imagine that it came forged from barbed wire fists that crackle in fire pits, adamant on burning any semblance of respect that I could ever have for me, and that in forcing my hand to take a wretched baton, they somehow entombed my dignity in the death traps of a moniker that I still refuse to own.

I may not know who caused such problems, but if I were logical, I would say that it was an ill-composed clone of my mother, as if she thought that tying me to herself by way of trivial sentiments would create a bond that nothing could break.

Sentiments of love that I never grew to appreciate

It became a pass-me-down heirloom like Isaac's blessings to Jacob, and it started off with my mother's mother, who never had a name to give to her children,
and my mother took it as an airbrushed consolation prize and gave it to me as a way of wishing to remind me of role models who weren't perfect lessons to begin with.

but somewhere before the average child could speak, she took to contouring every detail and pronunciation of the letters "O" and "K" and blended them together so that I could learn to answer to the smoothness of an alias before I learned that I was one thing at home and another outside, and I realized now that they could not live with the aged name that lay in their mouth like broken light wires assaulting flooded streets, so they gave it back to the system, one of whose pillars taught me that I couldn't have pride in it because it would be nothing more than a joke in the hands of children like me.

So I vowed in my heart that one day I would do a deed poll
and find a name suitable enough to match me.
one that they could never make fun of.

Permission to laugh

When Rachel Wiley told the fat joke, I looked to my mother
for permission to laugh so I wouldn't hurt her feelings.

Wouldn't make her another shadow of dysmorphia and 'yo
mama' jokes

Wouldn't make her pain psychosomatic and diet
Wouldn't make her society patient and gym fanatic
Wouldn't make mockery of her making fashion shows with
clothes from her slim days just to see if they still fit

And she stayed silent, as if breathing in all the insults gained
from reminiscing.

And, I remember the first time I described someone as fat,
remember how she curled herself into a scolding, how she
spilled over folds in caution
She said that the word fat was disrespectful,
looked at me like she couldn't believe I was who she
extended herself into a nine month pentagon for
spoke to me as if warning of ancient sins only illustrated
in Moses' laws
and every time I used the adjective of abuse, her heart broke
in her eyes

When I laughed at the fat joke, my momma twisted her
tongue together as if biting back cries and I became bullies
she didn't ask for

And I can't remember her every being slim, but she got pictures she swore were right before my escape

Proof that it was me that made her this way and I laugh at the fat joke not because I want to, not because of it but because of how uncomfortable a silence I consume whenever I have to describe her physique and my momma hates the word fat and I can't say she is well-rounded or spherical or big boned so I mention Rachel Wiley's fat joke and hope her doctor becomes satire and humor and sensibility and she feels better about the word fat because she is far more than just compressed nerves and 3 figure digits on a scale

Let me introduce you to my wildest dreams

I don't know what the soft woman era is, but I've gotten so comfortable talking to fictional characters that I don't think I'm meant to be around real people. I'm not smart enough to comprehend affection and displeasure, and I don't fit in the world I've encountered.

See, I don't do holidays; celebrations aren't my forte, and I hate the whole birthday shindig.

I'm the common denominator in a lot of problems, as if I'm a negative magnet lining troubles up to fall like dominos.

But somewhere deep down, I know I wasn't meant for this world, and if I'm a mistake, how come I still hear heaven's dial tone when I leave messages on read?

In my wildest dreams, I find it funny how I wanted so badly to be here for the end game and throw a touchdown in the last quarter
So I could see myself spending eternity riding in the passenger seat of vintage cars, ignoring oil spills and locker room sweat.

Yes, that's what heaven means to me.

So if dreams did come true, I'd be lighting cigarettes while driving down backwoods streets that I don't know yet. And I wanted you to see me headed to gun ranges blasting classical country music as a tribute to the 80s, 70s, 90s.

But dreams are mystical things that are never fully worth it, and I'm a Gen-Z girl that still can't see myself living here, and if reincarnation isn't real, how do you begin to explain my jigsaw piece fitting into the old world?

How do I explain?
I don't like technology, but I love movies and books I don't like music or seeing things in color, but it's a blessing to have sight, and I'll dance and learn the words so they won't see that I'm an alien resident who's not truly worth it.

Maybe I'm born in the wrong place and the wrong time, so find me a necromancer to take me back to the days when people didn't have to socialize, or better yet, let them diagnose me with narcolepsy, and I promise it would be the highlight of my being.

Because when I see pens dying and papers burning, I know the ban of books is not worth living in this time and this gift failed to teach me that poetry is really dead and prose was for Dickenson and Brontë, but can you blame me for wanting to be trapped alone in the 70s?

I want to be trapped alone and in the 80s I want to be trapped alone in the 90s, and maybe I'll meet Marilyn, and gaze upon beauty I have no hopes of achieving.

CHAPTER V
Poetics of Society

William Shakespeare's 'As You Like It':

"All the world's a stage, And all the men and women merely
players;
They have their exits and their entrances,
And one man in his time plays many parts,
His acts being seven ages.
At first the infant,
Mewling and puking in the nurse's arms."

And the caged bird sings

When I found out why the caged bird sang, I stuffed its song back down its throat should anyone capitalize on the bronze nodules hanging to her vocals. I told her to garnish my self love like it was an old recipe, make me regret romanticizing suicide like I could salvage apart of my identity.

So, when I fell in love with the poem instead of the poet, I told the caged bird to serenade me like I was an African drum, said to beat into me like I am the weary heart of the jungle whose nutrients no longer float in her land.

Told the poem to water-ceremony its European verbiage into a fluidity I could understand.

When I found out why the caged bird sang I told her to do her worst, to make my memory form an indentation on your heart that no matter how lost you get you can always find your way home by remembering my name written in the walls of your chest, so imprint my thumbprints as the key to the 24 bars imprisoning your heart.

When I found out why the caged bird sang I took my time relearning the calls of the blue jay so I could love again.

When I found out why the caged bird sings I folded all my pieces to my chest and said I'd rather see you leave than see me wrecked 'cause I'm not the type of girl to nurse your burdens and give you rest more like the type to cause you stress and call it blessed.

When I found out why the caged bird sang I tried to remember if the last time I said your name it was in a dream or a poem.

My sister

so loud she makes the volcanic eruption of Krakatoa seem like black hole waves

Her echo bounces off concrete walls, enunciating fully-seasoned lingo to stomp on necks so she can earn her place in the world.

an intolerable attitude bound to get a shoe thrown at her

Yeah, her tongue reflexes got her playing dodgeball with her future. And they call it disrespectful, but this rebellion is nothing short of a legend's tale.

My sister is Phaethon.

My sister so headstrong, she took death in her hands, said two words, and melted its ambition, and she doesn't even know that the stars deserted the skies to watch her shine.

My sister carried hurt longer than a nine-month love growing in the womb. She flung it across her back and dropped a piece of her pain, her blood, her tears, her bones, her fears, her...
No flung it over her back and left a cacophony of bitter words in her stance. Now everyone is choking on the truth.

My sister so furious her loud takes a backseat. So that the cries of this little girl are heard.

So that her feelings are made valid. But we are all hurt hurting each other.
All bleeding different shades of pain, refusing to use it to build the other. Too consumed by our own travesties to even notice [20]that she was loud to get her voice back because she wouldn't know its own melody over a megaphone.

My sister so loud; she is both delight and danger.

My sister so furious, she takes council with Eris, Atë, Kali, and Medusa.

My sister so vengeful that she still finds bitterness a soothing companion.

---

20 *"How do you survive whole in a world where we are all victims of something?" A profound question posed to American novelist and editor Chloe Anthony Wofford Morrison (Toni Morrison) at the Connecticut Forum on May 4, 2001.*

Her mother?

I met a girl who loved sociology, said she loved conflicts, but Goffman is her favorite theorist. I didn't believe in the study but stayed to watch her tell her story, contemplating the bitter truth that we are all actors, and if that's true, then her momma is the greatest showman of all time.

She deserves a standing ovation for keeping dramaturgy relevant. Stunting like she's the best this world has to offer, that's pathological. I came to understand that spittle ain't the only thing coiling around the lies in her mouth, like they were porcupine pins aimed at her kids' hearts.

Because, though she doesn't say it, her love is contingent on everyone around her being a cash cow.

Milk you till you're bone dry, then it's normal to say bitch-bye. Start a fight so the distance gets wide and the time frame feels tight, feels right hoping they'll be mad enough not to ask for their coins. See, her children, they're used to this fight. Her oldest has been living it all his damn life.

White knuckles clenching fists because he ain't mean no disrespect, but he paid the way his whole life, so why's he still feeling trapped in this net without boundaries? I said the shit's pathetic, she got her children cutting umbilical cords with the jaws of life held high when they accepted that she was more of a mystery or memory, like Aunt Jen.

She said her mom's biggest performance is currently unfolding, like her eyes staying closed to the trauma she pushed towards them. I laughed and said her momma was a stumbling block; her side effects sound like she's addicted to dimes like it's crack. I said living out your means yow, that's wack.

I can't imagine knowing someone like that.

She scowled like she didn't want my opinion, then she said "yo mama jokes don't hurt, I'm numb to the embarrassment" but she's beyond all that, I said "great ain't no use taking shit seriously with a mom like that."

My mother

is steel-glazed love mixed with the warmth of honey to make abandoned buildings home.

My mother is an abandoned barn, is farm animal for slaughter and sacrifice in place of the children who have vacated the lot of her body.
She is ocean wide with hips of ashes and bullets, should the Bible not be enough axe to protect her soul and those she carried

My mother is modernized tradition.
Is I will not see my children do illegal shit and stand by their sides, but she is not someone with the power to walk away.

My mother is Rhea flowing amber through the veins of her swallowed children to make them strong enough to wield sabres and brave enough to walk behind their own shadows. My mother is the deep, flowing river of Erie that stays still on occasion so that we can wash our sins into her with little judgment.

My mother is Proud Mary sniper-ready, and Queen Latifah's feigned death in order to set it off.

My mother is a woman who is not selfish enough to say no Hardworking but not smart enough to save or have a proper plan.
My mother's impulsive tendency, wrapped in gourds of

scripture, is hatred for the husband who have used the coffin of her womb as a pot to sow his oats. My mother is the difference between a fairytale and reality.
Is the meaning of "si mi an live wid mi, a two different ting"
She is hallelujah tongues one second and hell's fury the next.

My mother is an electrocuted barbed wire fence no one can climb over. Is the character not main enough to make it to the season finale
Is grandmother loved but choked by ailments
My mother is a gambler between salvation and sickness.
My mother is lungs tied outside her body to be assaulted; is strength given when alone; is history implemented in medical exams; is love injected into every deltoid muscle; is last will and testament for her children because all she has to offer is herself.

She is a concert pianist, surrendering the best parts of herself to add to the missing pieces she can still spot in her kitchen.
My mother is the little ingredient in baking that makes it good like cinnamon and rose water, and you never know what is coming next.

A disaster or a pleasant surprise

When I said I had no home

I forgot how my mother's body would feel watching me parade myself with a shadow of her bones behind me, a red sea weaving carpets for my induction into society.

And I say I have no home, like the reshuffled lot of her body was never on lease to me. As if I don't owe her for the things I broke when I stayed there.
Like I am not an unwanted intruder who pried open her legs like they were castle drawbridges.
Or red carpets flowing for my arrival, I don't know which it is just yet. So, when I say I have no home, I wonder if she turns herself inside out to remember what she looked like before I left her bare like thread-worn tires and curved rims. Before I left her, searching for evicted housemates to find her worth in their eyes.
Her happiness in their success.
Her youth in their offspring.

When I say I have no home,
I wonder if she has sudden bouts of malaise.
If she reminisces on the months I spent constantly reshuffling her body to make me a home.

To build me a casino of security, and I've been focused on moving things around ever since I left that I never took the time to stop. And I was the worst pregnancy she ever had. And the only one to claim myself as a nomad. And my mother's body, beaten-down shelter as it is, begins to regret the elasticity wasted on me. As she sees me sully the name of her home for a temporary dwelling place I will never be comfortable in.

Estranged Family

Ever since I laid eyes on you, I began to play blue clues, because I never truly understood why you were missing from the picture in the first place. And when you finally came around, I heard stories from common miscreants that had me thinking you were a better mock-up of a Kardashian's BBL.

Watched as each time you visited, you set fire to the mosque they rebuilt, turning each stone upside down like a ritual to induce amnesia and as a child, I didn't realize this place called home could be Seinfeld's own hell. Where the hydrants from the Bible are gasoline-filled and each ward made peacemaker, made firefighter, say there is no fire quenched by back talk and rebellion.

I'm older now, but not necessarily wiser, so I have a vision board that sees me as an estranged rookie, sharing your modus operandi

Teaching me to only visit when Jehu, son of Nimshi, crashes horses into dovecot hearses
then gather in black veils, seated with former generations of family homes, paying our respects in pews and singing holy verses as vervain incense lights another body, hoping this is enough to realign chakras and courage. I haven't gone back in a while, and I think I forgot how to use Raven Symonè's vision to see you rumor roulette jockeys to turn the tables back in your favor.

Somehow in all the lessons we learnt and rebellious moments, we never learned to pick our poison.

As if doing so will make up for lost time instead of serving revenge on an open rotisserie fire.

And if this isn't déjà vu, then I don't know what is because I still have a vision board where
I've watched lies of omission consistently curl themselves into commas caught up in the dinner speeches that turn laughter into arguments. Turn the past into bubble-wrapped knowledge once pushed away for storage the day we left behind these places, these stories, these dead end relations, because we don't want everyone to know that we're all somewhat damaged.

That there is a broken child in each of us that these self-made infidel parsons committed before eroding limewashed flesh to the burial.

Now I've emulated you, visiting on occasion because I can't stand to see how messed up they made us. Yet, they say family sticks together, but blood and water only go so far if you make it.

And I have better things to do than sit around and reminisce about broken compass-cloned pocket watches that fail to show that tradition isn't worth it. That water can do damage, but
Blood is a magic that tends to consume without reward.

And just like you, I've warned them too.

If they leave this bloodline in my hands, it's going to die with me because I'm done contributing to wardens that got hurt and think that's the perfect lesson plan on parenting.

Tough love makes a soldier, but we never asked to be soldiers; we only asked to be children who were loved unconditionally. The problem is that familial love always comes with a condition: do as I say, or else.

Hurt

I've got a friend.
That's trying harder to hide the pain she buried deep.

sawing between flesh to see what lies beneath

And her tongue is so used to saying that she's fine.
I don't even know how long she's evaded the truth to coddle
the lie. Sometimes I look, and I wonder if she notices this
isn't normal. I wonder if she cares that the alphabets forming
words in her mouth are bitter on the tongue.

wonder if she tastes her own tears as they shatter on the
floor.

Because even when she's drowning on the inside, and her
smile is falling.
She wouldn't be able to express how she's felt.
And I want to do all I can, but sometimes the people worth
saving need a savior who can hold their own light in the fog
of darkness, and I have stumbled too many times on the
bridge of uncertainty.

So, I can't really help her if her story is still hidden beneath
the hieroglyphs written on the palates of her heart
So, if you're looking to help her, then

I think it's buried somewhere where Moses broke the stones.

she's still in the desert crying out, *gentle Jesus meek and mild*

But I can't mend her anymore, so I'm hoping he's got the first aid kit that my hands won't open.
I spoke a prayer for her today and told Him that I'll help her stand, but I can't do much anymore; it's impossible for me to tell her to choose a better path when we share the same lane on one dead-end track.

I've got a friend.
Who acknowledges people who are grateful for life?
She once told me that these people are optimistic, and that makes them brave because every opportunity they get brings tears to their eyes.
And she couldn't understand where they found the strength to make it every day.
I remember looking at myself and looking at her, thinking, "How could she, or me?"

When she's still waiting on a blessing, that seems 15 years too late. So, understand how thirsty she's feeling.
How deprived of everything this world has to give, and it's like her day from hell never stops rewinding with different chances for mistakes and reflection.
I want to tell her that though those flames engulf her, I never want to meet her in a morgue, but I can't make a pinky promise when I may not be around long enough to notice.
I'm sorry for the day I don't notice.

Lasered off Medusa Semicolon

Someone said they don't understand the meaning of my art.
I said my body is a temple, but it's a museum of priceless
artifacts all the diamonds couldn't equate to

See
I've got a semicolon on my wrist telling me to keep going
and a flat line on my left breast, resuscitating my code blue
moments. I've got a Medusa on my thigh, freezing men to
stone should they think to raid this harvest. And I'm pretty
sure I've got the cross tattooed somewhere on my heart,
just in case the sleeves of my soul won't wear it.[21]

I'm still afraid that it may be the mark of the beast, so I
searched the Bible for what the gospel sought to preach
because I can't be a freelance writer when I'm constantly
judged at Jesus's feet, so I got the markings to give me hope
and prayed that these inscriptions weren't given a different
meaning from the identities I choked out of my childhood.
I've never been so focused on finding meaning in the truth
of the spirit because I know my God can get livid if I strive
to live by the flesh, so I do my research to keep his grace
from ever departing. See, I play my cards close when it
comes to fighting sin and eternal damnation.
And I've been going through the motions lately, trying to
laser these cat marks that my damaged brain pasted all
over my hands and thighs.

Now

I don't have a soul to cry to, so my art is on the organ I can't scrub clean. I wonder if these inscriptions hide the pain and grime from his hands, and the scars they said won't ever go away. I'm still praying that the questions stop in time for me to regain control of these habits I've quit.

I'm breaking down, and my 911 isn't answering. I guess I pushed emergency contacts too far away; they no longer hear the sirens. If I wake up in the morning, will I be angry that I made it through the night. It seems like every day I'm upset that I made it this far because others didn't and they wanted to. How is it fair that when you don't want something, you get it?

Did you know that I'm trying to pretend like life is worth living and it's all in my head, but faking getting better isn't worth it when each breath I take feels like gasoline shots in the vein?

Is this the beauty of life I should thank God for, or will self-searching and overthinking just spark another conversation with God? I want to know why Elijah's prayer is still on the land. If we're not to be depressed, how do we ever win?

21 Semi-colon: A first-hand account of conquering obstacles, especially those pertaining to mental health and suicidal thoughts or attempts.
Flatline: A profound loss or emotional death, numbness, or a life-altering event brought on by severe trauma. In essence, it symbolizes the absence of a heartbeat.
Medusa is intertwined with that of sexual injustice towards women more explicitly than men, Medusa represents feminine empowerment, survival, and strength, especially from sexual abuse.
Cross: a close personal relationship with a higher power or religious belief, in this case God. In addition to sacrifice, the cross
represents unwavering love, peace, commitment, and acceptance of salvation.

They said I could be anything

but they left no other instructions to follow, so I opted for
my best while battling mistrials passed down through the
cane fields of my ancestry. They said to draw a family tree,
but I don't have the best description of my family, so I've
been re-enacting August 21, 1791, trying to find one voice I
lost underneath the barracks of the white lion.

I couldn't trace my ties back to screams from broken homes
that still travel across oceans, so I filed for
for custody of my skin in Vatican confessionals and proved
that I was my own person, just in the skin of many nations.

See, I was one, but over 10,000 nucleotides crawl through
the pipelines of my veins.
Causing me to strip the barcodes from my chest to pay
crooked lawyers for refusing to accept the taxes placed on
the talents I haven't used yet. Yes, I'm still behind, catching
water in my hands and saving food for the seasons I most
dread. I've got dried blood on my back from where their
whips severed the tracks of my wings.

And I still have nightmares of conversations on hold that
last for seconds at a time when I think that, unlike them,
I'm in control of my life, but just like them
I'm bad at communication, and
I'm a creature of habit without a habitat to inherit.
I have lions taming me and cheetahs riding alongside hares
with how much I flip through the days as if I can't find a

lane worthy of my attention. I know I'm limited, but success is never an option, so like the wise virgins, I keep my oils with me because I can't be caught slipping when I only trust myself to keep my place in line when the profits start rolling.

Back through the years

I want to go back to 2019. When my heart didn't protest my every desire and
I could still hold my memories in my hand to erase the tragedy of art from my eyelids. I want to kiss my scars goodnight and feel safe in your arms once more. I want to go back to 2019 and write a letter to my apocalypse, telling her to take it easy on me because I can't fight another war without falling to my knees.

I want to go back to 2019 and breathe healing through my lungs before they collapse into the twin towers.

I want to make art so seductive that it will take your breath away. I want to be seen and heard. I want to be whole. I want to go back to 2019 so I can hug myself and tell her she's brave. I want to hang me in museums so I can show her I'm the main character in the stories she has heard. I want to breathe. I want to freeze time so I can forget what loss feels like. I want to breathe. I want to walk the streets and make a mess. I want to smile with my heart, not just my chest. I want to go back to the days when I was truly at my best.

Gaslighting Religion

I always wanted to be a lawyer or a profiler, so on the day
I saw the writing on the wall,
I began to examine each piece of blood evidence I left
behind so I could find another meaning in the visions Daniel
interpreted for Nebuchadnezzar. And for days, I walked in
the confusion of Nicodemus trying to analyze the parts of
my personality that needed to be baptized. Because I didn't
want someone else knowing that, like Gideon, I had asked
God for confirmation of his word three times while
I taught my breath to count so that I wouldn't forget the
strength it took to stay alive.

I taught my tears to alphabetize each series of my emotions
and my hands to stay gripping onto faith like they were the
coins of money changers in the temple
I thought I could stay in the church while constantly wishing
for the pleasures of the world, and my flesh tells me that it
could follow me through heaven if I gave in to my desires.

So I gave my mind subtitles to get away with sinning as if I
could trick God into believing that I followed all the Bible
when I tried summarizing his narrative, and I became my
own attorney in the judgment, prosecuting each verse as
if I had a say in what salvation meant.

Story of the drug dealer's daughter and love

When asked why she does not love, the drug dealer's daughter said that she believes that love is fool's gold. That she is the attempted resuscitation of a language drowned in Lake Baikal, a warrior fighting hemodilution without stopping to remind us that sometimes when love has nothing to hold onto and no purpose to belong, she starts comparing Delilah's betrayals to those of Judas', and she chooses the storyline that leads to ventricular fibrillation every time. To her, pureness is not synonymous with survival but an asphyxiation of devils lurking in throats to the rhythm of defeats hidden beyond the ozone layer because love, when rejected, does not retreat but instead recruits and trains those who never kept her from leaking from their side.

The drug dealer's daughter said that if she were a poet, she wouldn't use a beard as a rhyme to shield her reality from its rawness, but like a cannibal, she would display the truth hidden in the love of Cato and the obedience of Portia as she embraces the blood color her father hung around her neck from birth, notifying crips of her royalty.

The drug dealer's daughter said that she has gotten used to telling the stars her last words and staging catastrophes of falling in love because everyone knows it's a matter of time before the enemies of the drug dealer come knocking at the heart of the daughter, and she does not want attachments caught up in the crossfire she has no means of preventing.

The drug dealer's daughter said that this is her birthright; she too must become an avid baker formidable enough to push the skills of her father through every home in their community. The drug dealer's daughter said love is a grab bag of jobs that could see you dead.

The drug dealer's daughter said that sometimes,

She wishes Stars were the only gunmen who could hear the last words of anyone on the brink of death. That the love stringing up the history of her ancestors is enough lesson to break the chains still holding her hostage to the sins of her father.

She said love was a hustle not worth the commitment when the snitch-bitch codes of her father rang through her ears and pillow talk was the slaughterhouse of many men who, like Samson, couldn't keep their mouths from climaxing with their d***s.

Because I wear my emotions on my face, she looked to me for the questions I couldn't hide, but I just said that it's weird how we know that one day they will be gone. Yet we sanctify and preserve their memories as if their lives were really perfect.

What about the things they did to people who truly never deserved them? You blame a lack of love on someone whose affection was tied to the streets and how much money they brought in so much so that you keep skipping around the truth that one day the power of the drug dealer could be washed from this earth. You say you don't believe in love, but what else could make you a walking tribute to his life?

Moon flowers

Blotting shadows cast by coarse hair, gives rise to a woman,
a name unknown to foreign tongues whose body is no
stranger to straying hands.
Too familiar with the deafening sound of crumpled dreams,
like crushed bills pushed into pockets.

She was too blinded by those who wanted to profit off
the packaged products in her chest, turning dreams
into vulnerable victims of death and she shuddered,
remembering it all.

To him, she was number 2501.

her limp body a temple under white sheets, legs sustained
by gravity,
birth waters erupting so often within her mouth, cords
tugging at the strings of her heart, rusty tongs deep enough
to uproot trespassers and she had muted all screaming long
enough. to whisper, Rest in Peace!

She lays roses on mahogany surfaces far too often to ever
be counted. bidding the time those to come may return
the favor.
sprinkled wet cement on forked tongues and sped up time
so she would walk a bridge of redemption.

A sanctuary that saw sacrifices as victories. the dead as
tragic heroes and the infant within still questions her

motives.

Crying for mercy, his mother to save him. Accept his presence as her salvation.

He says she's forgiven. yet he's the one drowning.

She will not hear him; too distracted by

muddy rose waters marring her tired features in the stillness of the night for only certain women experience the effects of the Scarlet letter, the fevered kisses of stone against bare flesh

Tiger stripes tattooed into book pages illustrated by those who never knew of bruises

And did you see, did you see that steely glint within the desserts of her eyes? How its fathomless rage addressed the temple of Aphrodite and skeletons convinced her that death is beauty.

For a child must learn hardship on his own.

Society must drink the very waters of her dying soul. And taste, with salt, the cords buried deep below.

So, they may know her strength and stray far from those rocky roads. She is the woman haunted by ghosts of the future, and not those she once forgot to remember. Her devil was her decision, and the men who groped flesh with fire.

The wildflower questions convention

She is the definition of beauty in a cold world where blood
is just an exploitative term.
but
How long will we suffocate her?
How long will she poison herself just to please us?
She is so used to holding onto the hands of the dying like
the reaper himself.
Some days I wonder when we will begin to see that she is
under pressure too?
She is so far past the point of drowning, yet
You've asked her to give up another child before his birth.
Paid her in black veils and clothes for the day you'll finally
send him home in a carriage pulled hearse, but
I wouldn't... my mistake
I shouldn't expect you to notice because
She doesn't wear it on her sleeve. And
Everyone's burdens seem easier to bear than her own.
Darling, just own it.

If you deny yourself the truth of who you are, you will never
truly know the act of one imperfect soul carrying their
cross piled on the crosses of others and still seeking your
own worth with a bowed head. You've given life to the dead
so many times that no one blames you for being selfish once
for not all mothers believe that their children are properties
of country.

And those who ordered the death of able sons have never

gone to fight themselves.
Like the flower that bloomed in darkness, you questioned convention and bloomed where you were told you could not.
see
She is wise and everything angelic. She is Mother, a name she longed to hear from six feet three times

Mother, a name she will no longer give the dead For every coin has a rougher side. A side that was not polished enough too dreary or dull a side we hide all too often.
She is no angel.
But who said angels were the only perfect things in this world?

She is fury.
She is poisonous.
She is a woman hanging on to the life of another.

her swords are words, and her knives are pens.
she never aims them at feeble men's heads. she waits before plunging them deep into their hearts.
for
She has nightmares too of losing a fourth son to the chambers of gas.
Now in her selfishness
She cannot sleep, lest they pry him from her arms.
She makes me believe that some women see it as a sin to have boys in a world where wars never end.
I have come to understand that She is broken, just like the rest.

Pulling dark shades and sprinkling spirits over concrete without a tear for the boy she no longer knows but she became a hero when all else decided they couldn't handle this test. She does not lay her problems on you because you simply cannot handle her stress.
But she is under pressure.
She is drowning.
Allow her to be selfish for once.
Allow her to go through a day thinking only of herself and things beneficial to her.
Is her happiness too much to ask?

So,
Dear plebe, She is a warrior too. She has stopped sending
sons to die.
She washes blood like Lady Macbeth.
Spare her the trauma.
I beg of you,
Her mind is tired of fighting.
and her body is weak.
She tries to be strong.
stronger the strongest
She cannot hide from you.
You plague her subconscious.
She is on the verge of insanity, all thanks to your help.
You've handed her over to depression.
But her battle cries,
her tears,
her sweat
Her constant pleas

are proof enough that you cannot best her at a game she
is amused at.
Just give up
Laying low will not help when you slowly rob her of
precious moments. I wish it would stop.
That one day the earth will whisper back
That the blood fertilizing it will flow through reservoirs
That the child in her arms will forever be in her sight.
Just this once, let her be selfish.

CHAPTER VI
Black Majik

"The only curse you carry, her mother said, is the dark skin I passed on to you. You gotta find a way past that skin. You gotta find your way to the outside of it. Stay in the shade. Don't let it get no darker than it already is. Don't drink no coffee either." [22]

~ Jacqueline Woodson, Another Brooklyn

22 "Our melanin will always make us marvelous... Just imagine what that sea of sisterhood would look like.
Magic!" ~ Alexandra Elle

Passing while white

I never saw someone pass as Black until I heard of Rachel Dolezal. I never saw them, firsthand ride our coat tails from memes to global headlines potentially discrediting the hate they give us by walking in our skin without the casualty that comes with gatekeeping ownership over somewhere you don't belong.

I never saw someone throttle the costume of my race underfoot so they could map out the parts of my ancestry they wanted to keep, as if my melanin was a conduit for research,
as if she could just reach the zipper on her spine when she wanted to claim two races and become all-knowing of the tribulations of taking hate and handing it back out when she was not in character, Sophie Deveraux would be impressed. I wonder if I, too, could profit from my knowledge of being Black. If I could discredit the falsehood of her work If I could sue for public mischief, for identity theft, but I don't know where to go in the law.

I wonder if she knew the outcome of Black people masquerading as white? I wonder if she saw how the passing of passersby left an indelible mark on us.
I wonder if she knows the history behind the passing? Because I do.

I do because I have no other choice but to know everything that affects me or have the possibility to.

I do because I have to know all my history so that I do not repeat it
I do because all my family is Black, because no matter the shade of my melanin, I still have to walk gently on the roads you don't have to be afraid of.
I do because my skin is still flimsy, flesh made peacemaker, made an experimental magnet
made both headlock and shield, made wild animal prayer...
made prayer for the day someone said that they had to do it because they feared for their well-being.

And maybe I should take it as a compliment that you wanted to be us so badly that lip fillers, wide hips, and hairstyles were no longer enough.

But sometimes I see mockery in the Jenner of your actions and I am pissed that history has indeed repeated itself just not with us and somehow with all the changes we still have no power over the outcome of the passing.

When Chimamanda Ngzoi spoke of the one-sided story

I never analyzed it in my life because I never thought I was so narrow minded as to think that way.
I never realized others would have a one-sided story about me. About where I come from.
About my skin tone and my ancestors.
About the strength and submission of my gender.

So when the women in my life were rough with me,
I used to look for my face in the tidal wave of their distorted mirrors. I used to check off the dilations of worry I contracted from death, like they were flying fish bones aimed at my throat.

Then I thought of how I would give my daughter a life of roses.

Would mural her into bruising the head of every double standard, slithering its way into her home

Would find her a congregation of women lilithing the vibrations of possession thick enough to wage wars with a dermal anchor, a congregation of open wounds shapeshifting into women placing solvent and brick on each other

Would showcase a train of women long enough to plait our way into heaven should it become a patriarchy with the changing times.

I would teach my daughter what Kipling meant when he said that the female species are the most vicious beasts ever created. I would tell her that no matter the skin tone, we are all varying goddesses with enough power alone to overthrow another Babel attempting to steal our thunder or disrupt our rhythm.

I will help her fold her tongue into origami figurines and stuff it between the pink of her thighs, hoping to stifle it where no one could call it contraband. Then I will tell her to move silently until she has to be loud, and God damn it if she does not know when it's time to be loud.

When my daughter asks why we use our power to uplift the ones who dare steal it, I will tell her of the pyrrhic wars, will teach her the way it has always been.

Will backstroke through the passages of ancestors and pinpoint the boats made from the spines of brown sugar sirens.
Will pick at an Afro sail so high that God himself speaks to the ocean through it.
Will floss death from my bones to help her identify a race and a gender that have more attacks than they do praise.
Will depo-provera freeze my daughter's blood inside her body before she starts to realize that this monthly 7-day purge is some kind of deranged ritual that God uses when he washes her ancestral ties to every woman who has bled

by the hand of a man,
and sometimes the pain she feels is mourning for the
greatness snuffed out.

So I tell my daughter to be careful but not silent
To never dim herself to the pretense of another for as long
as she is alive and Black, then she is doing every girl whose
face floats across her blood a favor.
And I hope that when she does go into the world in all her
glory, there is no man to steal the power within her by the
touch of a garment.

Beautiful

She kept waiting for someone to show her her face in the moonlight,
for polished obsidian to be her best friend, and to tell her that she was the fairest in the land without even looking on the inside.

I heard that her mother warned her about beauty and the misconceptions of the art,
yet it was on the lips of virile men that she hung onto every elementary firecracker that brought sparks to light her face, sparks to dance to the showtunes of compliments that made her feel worthwhile.

The thing is, we don't really love Black girls until they become women, and I didn't realize she was broken.

I didn't realize I was attracted to broken girls until she held my hand and asked me if she complimented me, and in her eyes I saw the scars of bullies. The Oreo jokes and charcoal references.

Kids the same shade can be cruel if they want to.

I didn't know the deep-rooted issues she held from the past until she told me that she finally saw what I saw in her: that she finally knew how to talk to fit the margins of this world, but she still needed to know if the outside was her best side, and I had to let her go, for she didn't see that I didn't believe in perfection, and she kept stoking the fire like Cleopatra with Antony.

I couldn't be her Antony confined to drinking chai tea in lounge libraries, and debating Malcolm X speeches to Hitler's preachings,
couldn't imagine trying to show her each day on the hour that melanin is beautiful.
And
Throughout the conversation, I came to the conclusion that either she got lost somewhere struggling for her freedom when the English came or her mind is still somewhere in Alabama in the 1930s.

Where shallow women see themselves watching reality from the underside of glass-bottom boats.

I loved her but not her mentality, and my love is conditional, so I couldn't love her like I needed, and it hurt that she didn't realize that Mandela waded through the Ganges so that we could feel like proud people.

I kept watching her hurt, thinking her beauty only shone when she greased her palms to braid her hair or coat her skin in cocoa butter and oil at a certain angle so she wouldn't be too butch. And she's not the average black woman,
but I wanted so badly to be her Samari and enlighten her to show her the best queens were dark coffee with no hints of cream.

The women I love walk with their heads held high, breaking
the necks of cacti and feeding on the diet of John the Baptist.
See,
the women I love echo the calls of liberty, fraternity, and
equality in their bones, and her hips are porcelain pipelines
for future escapees.

The parting of her lips drops bodies like pagan verses
should she see them use blue soap and curry, toothpaste,
and honey to patch the colors they discredit,
and if God is not Black, then how do I get her to believe that
the fairest women in the land are the color of the night?

I guess I'm just another man trying to make the best of
loving a woman like this.

Sun-baked and worth it

I thought I had it all figured out.
That what the history books won't tell you: I would live through and persevere by picking cotton to press into the middle passage of my cerebral cortex. I guess I really didn't have a clue that each time I feared staring down a barrel, someone else was prosecuted for donning a hoodie.
I think I'm tired of this reality,
but I still dream of fitting in so badly
that I tell stories to kids of fairytale heroes and villains all honey glazed and grilled in the heavenly sun,
telling them that one day I'll see our reflection on a Broadway stage, collecting rose petals for embracing a distressed community,
and then I realized it wasn't a drunken dreamer's tale anymore.
I saw Halle take the screen, just wanting to belong, and she dominated the world.
But even then, I knew it wasn't enough to erase the feeling that we imposed here, so I asked myself, "How do I give back this unfair invitation?"
I ask myself if Hitler's Aryan race is still alive, because I feel hunted every time I close my eyes.
Every morning, I dread the news because I know if I take a step into the streets, I'll see massacres just for surviving in the skin of royalty. I may be paranoid,
come to think of it,
but if it's too silent for a while, then I brace myself for the worst. See, we were dealt a raw deal.

Wonder if this slavery and the last end the same, with the genocide of a race with nothing to gain from scratching at the eyes of the system that betrayed us
as Uncle Tom eats scraps from plates that defined us
and I wonder if we are Esau's descendants serving Jacob's and awaiting the trumpet of rebellion as if Toussaint is going to come and save us.
But every time I think about it,
I see that we have to push through, take each whip as if we were porn stars in some kind of rough kink,
and just hope one day we'll hold enough power to burn it to the ground, and maybe that time won't ever come.
Maybe we will advocate and protest, sending our voices flying across tribes and nations just to earn a page in history books we know our descendants won't hold.
But if we can make it this far by pressing our fingerprints into the margins of the globe,
then what's to say that they won't survive new theories until we all see that we're all the same?

Horror movie

If I were in a horror movie, I would be the death of Cleo.
would be tar meeting asphalt,
lineage without acid burning the gaps in my face,
highways of lifetime warranties without bridged
interstates
be a language without interpreters.
be broken bottles, bar fights, and brothels
Be Tony over Grammy
Pulitzer over prose
be surgery over surgeon
beatbox, jukebox over disco
If I were in a horror movie, I would be dead before the
opening credits were finished rolling.
Would be black ink spilled over carcass
be a lesson in surviving your first day hoisted into the
unknown.
If I were in a horror movie, I would never want to be
me because that would be the most frightening murder
scene.

Questions of a child; answers to which I never learnt

Curious eyes gazed up at me in wonder, questions drowning in their seas.
And she asked me
How do you embrace your blackness when there is no one to cheer you on?
How do you know where you're going if each footstep in the sand is your own?
I smiled smugly, having questions of my own.
So, I asked her
How do you propose that I begin to teach a child a history submerged in pain?
A past that lit torches and rained blood for the purging of sins
Sins embedded within the burdens of our skin
We are a battered race, no doubt.
But understand, child, that we are not broken.
We can heal ourselves of wounds, society somehow forgot
I told her that I grew up hearing about a polite lady who refused to move.
The contribution of one man to the Harlem Renaissance and, oh, the greatest dream of all
I told her that I learned the same rushed lesson two weeks in February every year.
Lessons that I was told served to honor the sacrifices of those this land cannot forget.
The ones whose soul lay buried in the waters I drank and protected the wombs, I emerged from her lips contorted

in frowns of confusion.

Her question was still unanswered.

Anger seethed from her bones howling questions she seemed too afraid to ask

if this is so,

Why do you not take the time to teach me what I really need to know? Tell me why my skin is such a burden to carry and why my native tongue slithers from my sight.

Tell me why I don't know names like Ralph Bunche, King Mansa Musa I of Mali, Ella Baker, Fredrick Douglas, and Thurgood Marshall. I could call so many names, and you will still not know whom I speak.

Tell me, is it my history that you teach?

Or just what you were told to make me think and of whom to think.

Mother!

We live in a land where my ancestors swallowed their pride, while housing blood in their swollen eyes.

They nurtured a dream that one day we would be people who learned to love themselves enough to love them too.

But if you continue to hide their memories in the forests of your mind, aren't they irrelevant to you?

Is that why you turn your nose up? As if dismissing my claim to a land littered with the bodies of my people

How dare you sit back and watch them say we do not belong here?

As if they are holy, building temples and cathedrals on the very cemeteries we called our people.

Mother, I will not cut out my tongue like they did.

Will not cry Bloody Mary over a land I wish would burn.

God forbid,
Our people never got the chance to see their children live.
Or it will someday become me who will have to tell my child
that she will know how to stomach the stench of death in
the air, that there will be people who think she was never
made in the likeness of God?
Mother, will I have to instruct my sons to be careful of
pavements painted red with chalk outlines of what could
become their own bodies.
Mother, answer me this:
Should I learn my history from movies such as Roots and
Twelve Years a Slave?
How is it my job to teach me what I should have been taught
from birth? When will you open your closet and let go of
those whom you have hidden?

I shivered from the coldness radiating from her eyes;
whispered that I already knew
I knew that when a Black man walks, you hear the hollow
sounds within his marrow.
For he does not know himself.
When a Black woman finds out she is pregnant,
She wrestles with the gods to keep that child safe, but I
have not matured enough to realize that I cannot hide from
what will eventually find me.

She said, "If you do not know my name, Mother, then teach
me my past. Allow me to embrace who I am supposed to be
so that one day I can find my purpose here."
I reached out.

but I could not hold her
as she went to search the sky reverencing gods she never
knew.
And that little girl whispered words that would make
Goliath shiver in his boots.

She said this is for the little girls who want to know their
history.
This is for the occupants of unmarked graves whose names
I do not know, whose identities somehow resemble mine.
We have forgotten to remember your swallowed body in
the belly of Gaia.

Simply put,we have forgotten to remember you.

Title, For the occupants of unmarked graves whose name I do not know, whose identity somehow resembles mine, we have forgotten to remember your swallowed body in the belly of Gaia; simply put, we have forgotten to remember you

They often say that dead men tell no tales.
But I somehow believe they meant to say that dead men show no shame. Because it's easier to crucify the dead than it is to crucify the living.
Easier to tear them limb from bloody limb while their bodies are still hot. And isn't that just how predators want it? Swarming bodies like pagan tigers with bloodlust in their eyes?
I believe that's how Jesus died while he was still crucified.
So if the dead tell no tales then
I believe that they are the easiest to crucify with lies from the split tongues of men. because unless someone can defend themselves,
We tend to rewrite their existence to please us, and we are all somehow guilty of it.

They claim you are gone, but not forgotten, and I often ask myself why mankind prefers to comfort the dead with such lies.
And then I realize that even though it's been 186 years and maybe more since you threw yourself overboard ships that were meant to profit from your exploitation,
I somehow find comfort in the fact that you fought for me to be free, yet your name was never expunged from criminal

records.

but I do not know your name

or your face, just that I got my color from you
my kinky 4C hair and wide nose

And I think your trauma too was passed onto me like ancient
family heirlooms serving as trophies to periods in which you
longed to be free. Your paranoia is imprinted on my heart
like holes for vermin to hide in.

And I learned to treasure them. Because I occasionally ask
myself, "How do I thank martyrs whose collarbones served
as wells collecting water from eyes that weren't theirs?"
Eyes they wouldn't ever come to know, like the herbs left
foreign to me.
I believe they still see us.

believe that they frown and roll twice in their graves,
because they cannot comfort themselves with the ways
we behave.

And I wonder what their opinion of me is today?
I wonder if they think I was worth their sacrifice?
These women, who are dead but still carry the burden of
Atlas,
Women who somehow scoff at the 21st century system and
probably 2020. Because
They don't believe in the dreams of their men to procure

the American dream in nations so far from America.

I imagine how their skulls must rattle in their cages with the hearty sounds they call laughter, and I try to rehearse their laughter. Because mine
Mine sounds like rusty hinges on a collapsed door. The very sound I imagine death to sound like
And I don't believe my mother taught me the sound of their laughter; no one did.
And so, I watch these women blame the system.
These women who claim capitalism is a bitch striving to ruin the lives of those who work their asses off.
And
I heard them pass a joke.
They said capitalism slept with racism and gave birth to classism, and later corrupted politicians who don't believe in their gods.

But understand that these are women who have forgotten their names. Because society refers to them as statistics, as angry, inhumane people who disobeyed the laws of a "just society," yet they have miraculously retained their faith in their gods.

And I hope these women know that I see them more like angels to my rescue. I wish they knew how much my heart ached to defend them.
And scream that they had names like us, that they were protectors, not destroyers.

Don't you know how much I want to follow their example and overthrow the elitist, chauvinistic barbarians that constitute the repressive government?

How much I want to point out to racist individuals that my ancestors walked with the grace of Aether, who made them believe they were goddesses bending air to their will, and I hope they can smile and show worm-eaten gums when I introduce their memories to my daughters, so they may learn to endure the oppression of this century.

I believe it was Langston Hughes who claimed that there was a raisin. in the sun,
and I believe that these women taught us that Black girls are not scum. I believe their lessons were vital to my life. So, I will make sure my sons know that tiger stripes are to be worshiped,
that beautiful Black women were whipped, and their scars woven together to form the barriers of the wombs he emerged from, that his name was uttered from the grave, and I was told he had a purpose.
I will make sure he knows I tell him this because he should treat these women like angels.
Women who embrace a little melanin,
Women who society urges to apologize for expressing themselves,
Women who have seen too many breeched babies with nooses tied around their necks

See,
I realized that, though your name is forgotten,

No water could wash your existence from the face of the
earth. Because like Harriet,
I will pass your memory through the pneumatic tubes of
my veins. I will keep your identity alive.
Even if I may never meet you to whisper my name and hug
you for choosing to give your life fighting for me to breathe.
I pray your memory may never die with me.
And
I hope your turning stops long enough to realize, that I may
never get the hang of life.

like how they never got your native tongue

Maybe you can finally realize that I will disappoint you on
occasion, but you should know all that by now.
So, can you lay still while I honor you for being a heroine?
My existence is proof enough that you existed. I was girl
made Black ashamed.
Now woman, Black, and ultimately proud
So, may I never forget to remind my sons to remind their
daughters to remember your strength, for they will need
it if they intend to be Black and a woman?
Two sins in need of no confession.

And I pinky promise that I will never forget to remind
myself to never forget to see your face each day I stare in
the mirror, because
I am the most familiar stranger I may ever meet. And
This may be the only time I come close to knowing you.

Kiellettyjä Kirjoja

Somewhere in America
Someone is ripping pages and burning books.
Imprisoning the words that seem to comb their way
between teeth and tongue.

Somewhere in America
A caged mockingbird was shot 17 times for wanting its
freedom back.

Somewhere in America
Someone is putting books behind bars, and charging them
with the crime of the cold, hard truth.

Somewhere in America
Someone seeks to bury pages beneath the mass destruction
that is their soul.
Heaped them like firewood and counted the numerous
times they've had to censor reality, so that their children
won't be blinded by rage.

But what sort of society do we encourage
When we tend to place chrysanthemums on the spines of
knowledge.?
Encapsulating truth and rage as they see fit to hide from
God and man

You see
Somewhere, people are silently protesting.

Because the book that speaks their truth is hidden from
the world and thought to be wrong,
These people are bleeding the very pages that are forgotten
in the mist of unnecessary laws.

So,
Somewhere in America
Someone is at their wit's end.
Trying to reach an unattainable goal
To have their cake and eat it too,
So, they've locked away the lessons of The Great Gatsby.
But continue to sell the American dream.

Their golden teardrops sealing youthful faiths unseen.
And
I know that somewhere there is a yearning for the Age of
Enlightenment. A day when we can read Catcher in the Rye
without paying a price
But everywhere in America,
Children are fed fairytales from picture books. Because
God forbid the words of truth on thin paper are too much
for them to handle.

See,
It's okay if one child can live through it,
But God forbid that another has to witness the gruesomeness
of reality from the heights of their privilege.
So, somewhere deep down,
We're all wishing that, like black words dancing on onion
skin paper, this ban, too, will burn.

Response to the backlash of #BlackGirlFollowTrain

[23]I've been to the lynching,
where I forced myself to watch Black bodies hemorrhaging because we were taught we weren't worth it. I disputed that narrative.

So I kicked these stereotypes to the curb last Thursday. I said I had a gut feeling that we were going to make it one day, that we would have something they couldn't steal, but who was I kidding?

They would rather burn our Tulsa than accept us into their community, and they say "All Lives Matter," as if we said that theirs didn't.

or that blue lives shouldn't

they said that we segregated them from the boats they themselves placed us on.

See, they whisper that we are still caught up in the past, as if slavery could be forgotten just because they didn't do it, but involuntary servitude can resurrect in four states where Sundown Towns still blare us into submission.

Don't tell me they didn't know this.

Black women created not only life but also opportunities and have lived in fear ever since,

---

23 *In January 2023, a new social media platform, TikTok, erupted in an uproar following the Black girl trend. This is a response to all the controversy following that period.*

Because
We censor the realities we face to appease the algorithms
of society, but now we unabashedly thrust ourselves in their
faces because we need to be heard.

Like leukocytes, these oppressors who so graciously play
the victim have hijacked every opportunity we have had to
elevate ourselves with the mere excuse that they fear us,
as if they don't remember the Red Summer, as if Polk County
wasn't another form of mass corporation hindrance.

But it's our essence that threatens them.

It seems like we are getting too loud with the truth, as if
we don't have a right to freedom of speech, expression,
and the press.
They say Black girls following each other can do more
harm than good, and they look at this unity as if it's another
Haitian revolution,
as if we have time to cater to their feelings and not the
promotion and wellbeing of our people.

Now,
to the men backing these women with quivering lips:
We have always known you to be spineless, have always
seen vitriol in your eyes and ignored it, but not anymore
because we are taking back our power.

So, let me see the best temper tantrum you can throw,

or rather, let me add more wood to this flame for you to play the savior to those that criticize because we refused to invite you into our sister circle. And before you respond, remember how your mother struggled to keep you alive in a world that would rather swallow you whole.

A Black woman makes more sacrifices than any other mother because she fears that each time you go out the door, something may keep you from coming back to her, but she keeps risking it because that's all she can do. And if her love is strong enough, then it will be all the armor you will ever need.

I have stared in eyes of mothers afraid to give birth to the skin of a new generation of what could become a Gen-Z holocaust

Mothers who refuse to give birth to another cemetery
citizen
Watched motherhood become less celebration and more
of a repass
And she vows to celebrate him every day since he came
crawling from her womb for fear it becomes harder to
breathe the day his skin finally betrays him and dresses
his bones for a museum or a hanging house for salted
flesh
And her nightmares consists of the faceless butcher who
will take him from her
Of friends and foes with no distinct difference

A *mother's prayers*

A mother said, there is no segregation or discrimination in heartache; only another will know her pain, no matter the race.

Only someone who has been gifted pine boxes from the streets will see how every boy becomes a sacrifice to the butcher and every girl is made tame by these moments.

So when I gave birth,

I tied his breathing to my umbilical cord so that he wouldn't die. And I prayed protection for him in each candle that I lit. Because Psalm 23 and sprinkles of holy water were too heavy a burden of repentance to carry if I had to break any laws to protect him, and when he got to an age where he wanted to run in this free world of his choosing, I encouraged him to be armored.

Never argue, but take the moment to be alert so that he can survive bad stops and illegal searches. I wanted my son to be a narrator, a great storyteller and a warrior, so when I first heard his heartbeat, I dreaded teaching him the meaning of hatred and the correct stance to take when pulled over.

I told him that I didn't want him to reach with his hands for identification, but with two fingers while staying still and saying sorry. I want my son to be a narrator.

I don't want him to be afraid of breathing.

I want him to be strong but not too intimidating.

I wanted my son to be a leader, but I didn't think I could survive if I had to see him on a poster board.

I don't think I could stomach it if they had marches with the name I gave him, just to make the difference that Black people have been marching for centuries to implement.

I bet our shoes have the blueprint for these toy bullets they spit in the colorful phrases of each backhanded compliment and accusation. But I know one day he will have to learn what T.H.U.G. Life truly means, and that's scary if it comes after an encounter and he is left sticking to the pavement like overcooked pancake batter because he didn't know how to act out in these streets.

But at what age do you ruin their innocence? At what age do they stop being children?

Do I teach my boys with my girls, or can I tell my girls later on? Who wrote the book on Black people's etiquette in America? The unspoken dos and don'ts of a minority race.

So instead of waiting,

I'll teach him from the get-go that I want him to dress and speak so properly that he can make wine flow from water, and if he was respected, then they wouldn't see him as a threat.

But if my son can't be himself and embrace his roots, should he be seen as any less of a man by the people who resemble him?

I want my son to appreciate his roots and step on toes. But most importantly, I want him to live.

And that's not too much to ask.

Where I come from

When a Black mother gives birth in the ghetto
She becomes another suicide bomber, planting her hopes
and dreams in something she believes in
And that does not make her a fool, it makes her human
Makes her more aware of her surroundings
Makes her more warden than mother
More life lesson than friend
Makes her a great chef because she knows that one day
hunger will sink so far into him that his stomach will eat
its way to decomposition
And when he is old enough she will start practicing for the
day that he eats out
She will sing Negro spirituals and old gospel
Will paint that as good news and extra protection
She will learn to pray if she never did before
Will set herself a flame so that no one Soufflés him Miranda
while he is coated in a nose pressed into concrete
She will carry him in her heart just in case that Black boy
sees fit to force another set of blood diamonds round her
neck
From the day he is conceived she will employ credit cards
and bank books to pay rent for a tombstone she never wants
to use but knows it is a place where he will someday seek
shelter
And when she says her boy is innocent, watch them blend
seven minutes of heaven from the kush they claim was in
his stomach
Watch them cakewalk it down a powdered jury to find his

misdemeanor and she wonders if he is Moses or Jonah so she becomes both burning bush and trapped woman in remembrance of his memory painted on billboards so that everyone will remember a name she chose to never be forgotten
The victim, to a victimless crime

Prosperity land

They said that I could find luxury and opportunity in the
earthly land of milk and honey because the thorn-twisted
crown of Jesus sits atop the head of Lady Liberty.
And for fear of a deferred dream, I took the path frequently
traveled, praying that my raisin in the sun would be a
contemporary sonnet of fairy tales with happy endings.
But
When I came to America I piloted my eyes to keep watch.
Labored 24 hours a day to keep the bit from slipping from
my teeth and directed my skin to feel the tempo of the
wind in each hair that stood at attention, listening for a
conservatism prayer.
When I first walked off the plane to a land of many nations
serving whitewashed liquor to passing-colored patrons,
I started practicing my goodbye and repentance prayers
just in case I never had time to learn them in the midst of
struggle with the men whose job it was to serve me the
chalky outlines of death while protecting the public from
the threat ricocheting off my skin.
And
Each night, I weigh my breath to see if human life is now
worth more than 30 pieces of silver.
For
I could still see the blurred lines between sacrifice and
hunting,
And no one thought to tell me that somewhere along
history's lines we gave humankind as the ultimate game
and ritual to appease the grandeur of empires.

So, I pawned my voice for a personality because I don't want to be seen as ghetto if my enunciation and tenses come off wrong.

And I still put myself to sleep with the idea that my ancestors went to auction houses miles away to sell their native tongue for an opportunity they never got.

So, I believed that God hurts when he has to listen to our cries and see the bodies hanging like his son's, just because we chose to regurgitate the crimes our ancestors willed to us.

And it's not respect for the dead if it's generational curses for the ones we nursed here.

See, we are just trying to belong somewhere where our family never called home,

somewhere where our ancestors planted their greed in their labor, and plaited maps into braids hoping that in reversing my cards it would show James Madison that a handful of his ivory descendants still clutch the trigger of their tongues as if their Second Amendment rights were words that degraded other nations whenever their own skin needed validation from the threats a song posed.

So, each night, my heart races because the only dream with which we can succeed is not a dream but a nightmare...a nightmare where every road leads straight back to the doctrine Monroe left behind in the dust of his ashes.

And because I knew this, I started teaching myself how to breathe less threateningly,

Because there is a blueprint etched somewhere in my
memory of the world my people sold themselves to build.
I still daydream of Mesopotamian carpenters stealing
the craft of Joseph before Egyptian masons could beg
permission from ivory architects about the pillars they
needed to change,
because somehow the plyboards God placed on earth are
rotting from the salty sea water they dunked us in, and it's
best to do our part as stewards and arrest the past should
she repeat herself.

But this isn't a map that I have clearance to see.

Because these politicians think it's treason to speak up for
the change we think is due,
So they ban books that may open our eyes, proving that
their history is written by men who never faced death, so
let's just say that this ain't chattel, but it's still slavery.
Still, one man giving while two others rob you blind.
And if freedom of speech means segregation,
then the chrome in my lungs has festered into wounds I
never knew could be formed from words and ideas.

That's why I like the art that I can see, because ain't nothing
in this world that has the power to ambush the scribbles
left in the crevice of the wind. You see,
We didn't see the truth, in the pollution of the bodies lying
face down in floods that Jehovah never sent.
And if I spoke with my ancestors, they would tell me that
they too faced similar threats, but I shouldn't hold my breath
for reparations because that's not something I'm owed.

It's just another series of installments used to repurchase me. So if this is the land of prosperity,
How come all men are stripped white to the bone before being discarded in the fields?
And don't call it hard work for a better life if we all end up where dogs go to die before we can acquire the dreams sold to us and be told that we are finally worth it.

CHAPTER VII
Green Isle of the Indies: Xaymaca

John Lennon once stated,
that "Our society is run by insane people for insane
objectives. I think we're being run by maniacs for maniacal
ends and I think I'm liable to be put away as insane for
expressing that. That's what's insane about it."

I come from[24]

wooden pews, coffee-stained pulpits elevating preachers
condemning youths
I come from laws with hidden agendas
from Miss Lou dilect pan e map
so when Khori grab a rhyme u swear har spirit smile
from blood tainted wid storytelling but a leff Amina
Blackwood Meeks fi tell u dat
Ah God dis tan fram far ah fling weh couple talent so,
Joan Kenzie and Evy Royale dem deh two deh grab a lot
Sa Pearly grandson ca buss couple joke but Dale seem fi
got di kunchy pan lock
Guava haffi get him props and Lexi she woulda be the
bess if har chapta neva stap

I said I'm from backroad sellers to corner shop vendorsI
come from white livers and black lungs, lips painted to
match themI come from waves in stadium stands and
ocean banks
I come from nine night grievings to thanksgiving service
from "mannaz mek e worl go roun" to "igle jackass walk
ah tell dawg howdy"I come from everything being a
lesson or a sermon
I come from worship
I come from herbal medicine and bush doctors
from meeting houses to kingdom hallsI come from pride
of self to love of country
from 'Jah music' bubbling through cisterns to Olympic
championshipsI come from street corner bars and

butcher shops
I'm from prime time news to Miss Kitty being the
epitome of independence and success
from red stripe promo girls,
PTR Rebel Dis Rebel Dat
from Gaza and Gully serving as the initial reason for
fallouts between familyfrom pan di bank to Boglefrom
climbing trees and skipping rocksroadside cricket,
court football and d-cup matchorange and green wid di
wagonist dem fi match
I'm from the versatility of breadfruit

Wi fourteen parishes dem unique fi choo
everybadi have a different accent and dem chat bad u see
but kunchy people tek e cake
uptown speaky spokey and downtown just brawlin wid e
Portmore try fi b educated ah st e mek a language a dem
own

I'm from bars and Bible aligned so smoothly you can't tell
where one begin and the other ends
from a fruit e muss can juice
soursop and carrot dat a Sunday best
I'm from Chubby and D&G
from Busta and johnny cake
bulla and pear fi days
bully beef wid bread and cheese
from pink milk school days to ice cream bike pan Sunday
from unreliable tailors to dressmakers
I'm from breda Anancy to cat on the spinning wheel

from cartwheels, rope skips and country fresh trucks
pikney weh know how fi tun dem han mek fashan
from one patty split in two cause even a spoonful a wata
can share

I'm from English being formal but always broken
from cussing and support being the glue that holds us
together but prayer is in our blood just take a look at well
over 1600 churches
GOD fearing and unserious what a ting it is to be from
where I come from because it's always a blessing watching
the changes of the nation and the love we emit

Ode to Elaine Thompson-Herra

Fastest woman alive a title you earned tearing Achilles
tendons from years of discipline root canaling pain into
an exodus no one could touch sewed gratitude onto the
rusted spikes of your boots, see

When we issue flowers we tend to wait for death, sometimes
even then we may oftentimes forget so here is to a butterfly
whose wings are forever changing, in the heights of paced
flights a woman breaking records through multiple injuries
we talk about one forgetting to mention the other like this
ladder they climb ain't serving to make our nation stronger

so run Elaine run from sports day to Issa Grace Kennedy

From Diamond League to Olympic tracks, chasing Flo Jo's
record beating one in a legal wind. Making a name in the
league of the greats, exhaling the pain inhaling the gains.
I wonder how many injuries left you with an immaculate
stride you constantly strive to perfect, stuffing the mantras
from your schools proving that actions always stand on
business so you don't need to exalt yourself

You've been running on discipline since twenty eleven held
you back 2009 saw you place rural schools on maps by
cackling waves through the air and not just stadiums stands
leaving your name cemented in grace so when you leave
this race they'll remember the prayers falling from your
mark set those blinders on awards all this determination

25 *"I think one thing I've learned over the years is just that you're not going
to ever please everyone, and the most important person to please is yourself"
~ Elaine Thompson-Herra*

to be the greatest all you see is another best time to break not just a champion

You're our North Star a Flo Jo sprinter with a talent for the craft personally we don't know you just how hard you run and lately this country forgets to say thank you especially for the sacrifices you make putting your body through all that you do serving a country ignorant enough to play one side of the coin and another when your work no longer please them.

[25]So
Run Elaine run from banana ground to Jamaica's hope

Sprint Elaine sprint from home of champions to words not deeds
Run until your lungs learn to hurdle over itself

Lighthouse a destiny of excellence through knowledge on your chest.
Hear how an emblem of prayers dash from a single shot

How your heels take flight from Kirk Vine track meets to National Stadiums
How gold and brown shifted to gold and maroon how even that couldn't keep your sprints from prime time black green and gold

Reach into global stands grab that baton thrusted forward from Penn relays

Then run Elaine run from banana ground

Chase a legacy into your name a laureus into your awards
Until the ghost of your stilts leave a dent on those fifth lanes
Run Elaine run from Morelia to Glasgow
From Beijing to Rio, Portland to Nassau

Run Elaine run from Gold Coast to Lima Eugene to Budapest
Run Elaine run from accolade to accolade
Sprint yourself into six Olympic medals

Stand proud as the first female ever to get a sprint double
Then run Elaine run into an Olympic sprint triple
Run Elaine run into a dominance they can't forget
Run Elaine run they think these injuries mean that you're
finished but run Elaine run from high school lessons learnt
into a discipline that made you the fastest woman alive run
Elaine run for you've earned that right

I come from peace, where, if you look closely, you may see the goddess Tranquillitas sipping herbal tea

I'm from a place where brainstorms are for people who think they know but don't know that they don't know.
I'm from chimneys and pails.
From washing newspaper lined latrines in jaze to inside toilets

I'm from Hardwood benches adjoining desks

> Blackboard dividers and dog-eared learning posters
> From rulers used to introduce children to discipline

From aged pages rustling beneath fingers and termite-eaten shelves to store them

I'm from loud gospel music, drowning the cries of 94-fm rooster wakeup call.

From Banana leaves to tie pastry and poisonous food made national treasure
I'm from church on a Sunday morning, and hill and gully profile and nyamings
from action and the burger man,
From Itty and Fancy Cat on a Friday night.

Jenny Jenny, Dhalia Harris, Aunty Simone, Delcita and Bashment Granny Shebada days

Yes, I'm from jumping over furniture at the end of commercial breaks just to watch the black burns at Royal Palm Estate, cabbie chronicles and the stars that are always rising.

I'm from constantly backing out of plans even when I didn't ask, because I know the answer is a dream.
And big finga or duppy nuh tell lie, so if they see a fish, it will always point back at me, and I'm not ready for the drama.

But they can't figure out the dreams the dead whispered to them.
So, I think I come from a place that's built solely on pretense.
I'm from weekend, holiday Christians who turn sinners when their feet leave holy ground.

From finger-pointing community gossip to a village raising a child, just in case they think to cross a certain line.
From residential areas that turn gated when new levels of upper class gentrification begins.

I'm from teachers telling students about themselves because they don't need this; they already have a degree.

From school challenge quiz to JCDC and All-Together Sing

From national phrases to brawling cuss words. I'm from Grandmas and greats, doing all they can, and giving their last even when they don't know how to pave the way
from most daddies, either dead or missing, and those that stay sometimes not helping.

I'm from the illiterate, teaching their mistakes and drawbacks to people who don't want to hear them just yet, from the duncya to the educated
From the land of "Mom Luby and the Social Worker" coincidentally located next to "The Two Grandmothers"

I'm from a place that always has something else happening.
A place where ignorance is bliss and we take pride in not knowing its definition
A place I think is Canaan because the light is always shining.
And even if we are the cursed Israelites,

We make sure to find our ground.

I'm from many people made one.

But in this melting pot, we are all either colorists or colorblind.
I'm from a place where everybody has an aka: Blacks, Pinky, and Pearl from outta crossroads
From Miss Margert dung a kunchy weh nuh too like people chuss har goods to Maas Jacob calf a roll.

I'm from a place I like to call beautiful.
the land of wood and water[26]
A place you call heavenly because you don't see what I see when you come
You don't watch children fall from a bicycle and play skipping rope with belts
I'm from climbing trees and building swings,

26 Xaymaca

from river dunks and street raves
From mocking dogs to stoning them and running
From red ants nest unda apple tree
teas from guava leaves

I'm from likkle teasing, you may call bullying

Where I come from, you won't see it from your visits, because you see beaches and white sand between your toes, skylit nights, and not one house rearranged to confuse ghosts

I'm from a place where mosquitoes and mongrels are national pets
And it's believed that God placed the sun right above our heads to train some of us for a future in hell

You think you know where I'm from?
But you've never seen children build trucks from country fresh boxes.
Make kites that fly, play ring games to induce tummy aches, and listened to Anancy stories with eyes gleaming of interest

I'm from childhoods of proverbs and idioms
From jax to marbles
From slingshots to beer cork tambourines
from superstitions to signs and dreams

I'm from creative minds, where every artist is from the

ghetto.
And every success is somehow rooted in a sad story that half of our country know isn't real but still searches for hope and something to believe in

So we cling to what we see
We cling to having people who made it, so we'll make it too.

So, I'm not just from food or music,
I'm from the thing that makes us the capital of the Caribbean,
I'm Out of Many, One People
And yes, we fight and complain, but without each other, this reality show would be such a dud.

See
I'm from my own paradise, where even corruption and crime have made their home on the lips of politicians that we hold dear.

Legend arise (Ode to Asafa Powell)

The legend that initiated the race for champions
Cruised into two World Records
Stenciled his name on the lines of the greats
Carved out his ambitions on lanes whose winds heard his
worst fears and saw his glory days
Crossed that line slapping a 9.07 mantra on his chest
He said it best, he is truly the only one who can defeat
himself

So
Rise Asafa rise, a nation once watched with pride as you
took home both championships and injuries, allowing the
dust to billow at your feet like Saharan waves
Rise Asafa rise, a nation still watches with pride for you
were the beam that made them see how great our future
truly could be

Rise Asafa rise, retired but still remembered like it was 2004
all over again
Applauses for your years of bending your body to the will
of the sport
Rise Asafa rise, curate a career from raw talent and genetics
Embrace the realities, the accolades and more
Breathe in the love and support from those in your corner
and then

Run Asafa run, with the faith of ministers ushering angels
after you

Sprint Asafa sprint, into history books and memory banks,
for retired is not a synonym for forgotten
Reach Asafa reach, so far out they can't see when you leave

Anchor yourself to something akin to humbleness as you
spring your body across those lines
Hand off a pain no one else but your teammates will dare
to take as their muscles too sometimes ache
Swell yourself into a new beginning not worth handing over
pain to your limbs

But never break, Asafa, for there are wonderful things you
have yet to do

When you leave the watchful eyes of a nation
Smile Asafa smile, for you have made the difference
Have been the landmark
Have achieved what some may never be able to
Hold those records, remember that feeling, and still run
Asafa run

Chase a new dream with the family you love.
Build legend build, a new track for your life, and savor the
moments you cannot retire from.

Motherland Ageless at 60

I cannot tell you who I am or where I'm from.
I can't put into words the experience of waking to fast gospel tracks and the sordid smell of bleach. Or the tasteful dancing of callaloo on my tongue come Sunday morning.
I don't know how to describe uniforms altered to barely make the rules. And you keep asking me to tell you where I'm from.
So
What would you say if I told you that I have been paranoid since birth watching the nation I've respected be chastised for giving her palace as home to Moses so he could slay her sons?
I've walked on eggshells to learn her truth while sampling her treasures, should they become luxuries I am unable to afford as inflation rates rise.
I have crushed papers illustrating the distress of her amorphous form as she is stained with the sacrificial blood.
But as I watched her name change from wood to water,
I kissed her cheeks as she stood on benches, perjuring herself in the name of protection, so our politicians are not tried for arson while they reap the profits of the bargain.

Her harvest is no longer of St. Mary bananas and Trelawny yams; she doesn't find joy in the produce of St. Bess, Clarendon Park patty, Portland jerk, or tourist trivia. but is too focused on weeping for crime and corruption, and though it does not break her

Her back arches with each whip cracked at her beauty marks, for she knows she has so much more to offer to people who will not see her.

Why won't they see her? She no longer believes she is beautiful.
Chronixx said to smile, but she has only found a few good men to spare her wrath.
She was the first Aphrodite made Medusa. She said to come to her waters. I tell her I've seen rivers purer.

That by leaving her to die in the darkness, I found a better way, and someday I'll remember to give back to her. She said to keep my pity. She said that others have promised the same but glorify her only when they feel it's worth something. She said my feelings are valid, but I am not worthy of attaching myself to her name should I leave her nest desolate.

Woman I promise you, I am working for us both.
So dry your eyes and let me bring you home the championship, and I don't mean the medals you so deserve from athletes defending your honor or the praise others eye you with, for I know you inside and out and they have only visited where you are less vulnerable. I will make sure I paint these limitless roads of the world in the color of your pearls: black for your strength and your beauty, yellow for your hope, and green for prosperity. I'll make sure they know the stains of red are not needed and that these battle scars are only progress made.

We are many. I am proud of your sacrifices and your heartache, for you have proven to be an avid warrior and will not be broken.

The tears you cry today I pray with everything that they can wash the sins from your body. I pray the prayers we utter for your peace as we celebrate your 60th year of freedom are the best you'll ever hear, but
Amidst it all, I know we brace ourselves for the fears of your heart.

May you persevere for 60 more, my love.
Happy Emancipendence, my dear.

Ode to Shelly

We aren't there when your feet bleed, when you've spent sixteen years doing far more for us than you do for you.

Yeah, you get the praise and we kept the recipes tracking your life while you become one with the wind igniting flames to the lanes of Hong Kong straight to Paris.

You deserve the accolades and more, but sometimes reciprocity isn't a given and gratitude is so seldom shown and you gave your better years from Wolmers to motherhood.

A fashion icon brandishing her country as her identity, so they see the black, green and gold before they see you for who you are.

Accolades layering accolades, a legend doesn't even begin to describe your greatness.

So when you run from home, I hope you find shelter in the wind, in the notion that you're not alone 'cause 3 million stand with you no matter the decisions you will make, and you make us proud for upholding your values and our hearts ain't hardened when you stand for yourself because this country sharpens pride with pride.

And you're not boastful, so when you leave your Waterhouse roots we know no one can bully you. Because you're Jamaican, strong-willed and destined for the greatest this world has to offer, so whatever life throws you when you've completed this race, I know you have the strength to balance its accounts, but you'll always be the one we keep at standards no one can amount to.

And though we only know the orders that stand behind you, I know those in your inner circle show you how much you're consistently valued.

I know your mama still has tears in her eyes from the first time she saw you take off at the sound of a gun, know she will still hand you over to a country until you know longer want to be their Florence Griffith-Joyner

I know your son is proud he witnesses you making history while still teaching him lessons from a baton he may someday take from you.

See, your villagers are the ones who never forget that you're far more than any superstar and an emblem of hope for your people, and though 2028 may never see you on the blocks, you're still a champion no one else can top proving—from boys and girls Champs—that your dreams would come through

Eight podiums, saw you lighthouse a tiny island wielding the first Olympic gold for your country.

You're God blessed and whatever relay comes next I know that you'll sprint through it, 'cause that starting gun isn't the only thing that can send you spiraling through the hurdles!

So as you continue living your dreams at the end of this chapter, I know you'll still coach your way through your trials, 'cause if you gave so much for a nation, it's a flex how much you'll give for yourself.

You'll forever be the only relevant Pocket Rocket, whose shoes no other can walk in.

Vernacular

When I say I am from Jamaica, it makes me an endemic
species, makes me a target for the culturally woke who
watched Zuzu Mafia and know Bob Marley's lyrics,
Makes me an escapologist, teaching myself to remove the
boundaries of an accent I never knew I had.

It makes me the greatest exhibitionist, forced to answer
queries with a smile.
It makes me understand Jamaica being somewhere in
Africa and being asked if I'm sure...as if I wouldn't know
the geographical location of my own home.

And I am brought back to Chimamanda Ngozi's one-sided
story as I deflect from answering questions in the format
of Charity Ekezie. But no one gets the hint when you're
being nice, so I was asked where I learned to speak English
this well, and she was surprised when I showed her that
the webs of my tongue were buttons I used to code switch
from proper colloquial English to the broken syllables of
the place I call home.

And she nitpicked at the words she found tasteful enough
to serve as appetizers for her next Model UN meeting. I was
asked if I was from Africa or just plain Black, if the houses
in my country were as advanced as theirs, or if we had jobs.

Was asked to dance as if tapping for coins,was stared at,
like my tongue ties reminded them of acrobats.

Was told St. Kitts was on the border of Jamaica, someone said they drove from one point and landed in the next.

Was asked if "I'm sure" when they asked if I smoked weed, as if the thickness of the cloud from my lips wasn't claustrophobic enough,
and so I unzipped my melanin,
Tucked my culture under the swamp of my arm, and carried it like a mother carrying a child.

I excused myself from the media propaganda, and think that to love a country is not enough payment to memorialize the scapegoat of a defaced, broken dialect and hang it over my skin, hidden between the covers of poorly threaded white sheets and termite-eating antiques not fit for my home.

I try to enunciate the phrases they are most proud of without the repercussions of my hometown peeking through my words.
So when they say I have an accent, I play it off because I know it's just another accident waiting to happen,
And they pile up like passersby slowing to view vehicular crashes on an interstate.

My patois is not a language for loan or a talent trick;
My creole is runaway slaves surviving by retaining their identity through the mutilation of English vowels.
So when you hear me talk, do not take it as a show; do not appreciate it as a poem or a lover; do not look at me in awe as if I sing the greatest melodies ever.

My tongue is not a trophy for how many primate Black
friends you know, mon;
it is not a safe house for your counterintelligence attacks
on what I know to be fact.

How can you tell me that phrases I grew up on are wrong
because your movies and literature never did their due
diligence?

My tongue is not a lantern for your appreciation.
Is not a cheat code for your cultural appropriation.
Leave it alone, for it is not yours to discuss.

Ode to Alia Atkinson

After Porsha Olayiwola's Water

It is a known fact that most Black people cannot swim, would surrender to the water before they learn to walk on it or fight the currents, multiply the weight of their body to the sinking of the Titanic, think it's easier to succumb to a drowning than it is to jump into the deep end without hesitation.

How many of us are so scared to trust the very waters quenching our thirsts?

It's a marvel to see you hold medals at stands that fear limits us from sharing.
How great a victory it is to know you have become the daughter of Poseidon, controlling the icy waters, bending them to your will, breast stroking through their rage like you too have walked upon them without fear or favor.

How brave you must be for your mind to leave the petrified states of St. Andrew and dance with grace in bodies that are oftentimes so successful in burying melanin.
How is it that this is survival, not a half-drowned tale of accomplishment, not an account of fear pushing you towards the finish line.

Dear Alia, how do you drown a place that has only seen typical weapons?

Freestyle a stream from a proud nation, not knowing how much you have disciplined your lungs to go with the flow? How this career path navigated more complexities than mere tides?

I wonder if this tsunami of a pool cleanses you inside out,

if this embrace smiles a welcome only you can see below her surface.

Wonder how peaceful you must be knowing you have conquered something far greater than you are, simply because you were not afraid to try.

Have anchored yourself into a beautiful space, inhaled a burning elixir of pain, castrated its matter, and slaughtered its ambition.

How can you be defeated when you have mastered something many men dream of? When you have gone to war and came out a sheen of your enemy sliding off your skin.

Droplets making you the queen of a sport we had no vision of mastering; now you are an example to those that will come after.

Butterfly a lesson for Sabrina Lyn to execute and build on her own story.

Be the guide of the water that sees us greater than we were yesterday. For records were meant to be broken, but names were meant to stay and you have made a mark we cannot forget.

Dear Alia Atkinson,

thank you for making us believe that we are still a nation with great talents, and the future is dependent on the execution of the unique gifts we are still harvesting.

CHAPTER VIII
Unsent Missives[27]

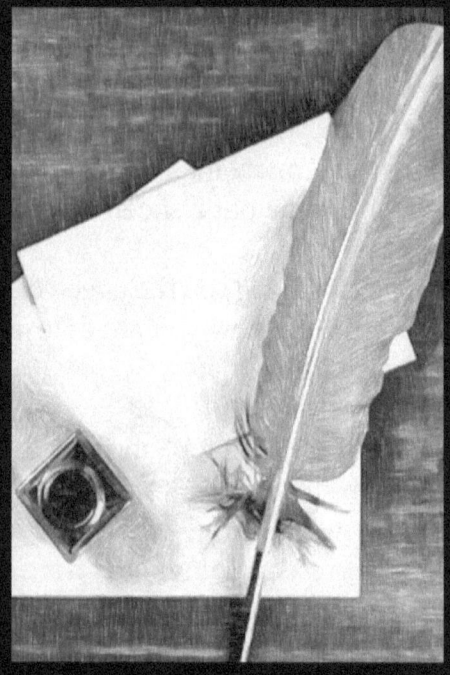

Warden Samuel Norton
*"...But you write your letters, if it makes you happy.
I'll even mail them for you. How's that?"*

~ The Shawshank Redemption (1994)

27 Brigitte: *"People write letters to the universe all the time...most don't get a response."* ~ Collateral Beauty (2016)

To some of my favorite characters

Dear Ntozake Shang, the rainbow is still not enuff when the quaking in my bones gives way to clogged arteries.

Dear Atticus Finch, I looked in the mirror and hung a mockingbird hoping to strangle the joy inside its throat before I could feel guilty of my own melody. And I'm not sorry, for it has done me more harm than a bluejay ever could.

Dear Elizabeth Bennette, I am still left judging your decisions of throwing away what I idolized you for.

Dear Benita Young, I too should be called Alaiyo (Al-a-yo) for I don't remember where I come from.

Dear Angelica Schuyler, I too will never be satisfied with where I am in life and the choices that led me to this point.

Dear Catniss Everdeen, can you teach me how to survive when all I want to do is 1945 my personal District 13?

Dear Annabeth Chase, I am still looking for the approval of my mother

Dear Sunshine, I too am coming to terms with the fact that Aunt Jen may have never intended to have us in her life.

Dear Emma, I am no longer embarrassed of Dory's narration

because I too have watched the lady at the train station become the pivot in the place I call home.

Dear Sophie Caco, I understand your culture shock.

Dear Lillian Ambrose, I am captivated by your strength.

Dear Hermoine Granger, I long for the type of friendships you cultivated.

Dear Daisy Buchanan, I wish for your wealth and beauty but never to inherit your dissatisfaction with life.

Dear Liz Murray, I admire your ambition.

Dear Ana Fitzgerald, I do not judge you but I still cannot comprehend the type of pain you must feel knowing you can only save one child by sacrificing the other.

Dear Sophia Charollette of Mecklenburg, when you are hiding from the gods do you sometimes wish you had gone over that wall?

Dear Anne Boylen, how did you learn to forgive even facing the guillotine, and can you teach me how to confidently cling to my faith when no one else believes in my innocence?

Dear Nanny of the Maroons, how do I become a pillar of unity and strength?

Dear Moleka, you are one of many standards I have learnt to judge men by, for how do you take the lessons of one woman to do right by another?

Dear Janine May Crawford, I too have seen death by the hands of power and known that keeping an eye out for God to take precedence in anything is paramount in success.

Dear Catherine Earnshaw, I too am misunderstood as stubborn.

Dear Clarissa Dalloway, your disillusioned mindset has flowed its way from the 1923 dust into my 21st century veins.

Dear Emma Bovery, I cannot say I blame you in the way you escaped the mundane except for your ill spending habits.

Dear healing journey, show me the difference between reality and my obsession with trying to dissect every character in each book, and the simplicity in just enjoying breathing the art form I love the most.

A lot like you

After Rudy Francisco

Dear Rudy Francisco,

I am not the average girl but I picked out colors that mimicked the sky on the day the savior died and cakes that sat so heavy on the tongue and in the stomach that it is no longer worth quenching the bitterness

By 14 I knew the time death would come knocking and the location that she would find me stringing my bones into profit

By the age of 17 I have already struggled with failure so much so that my plans become so dependent on loneliness

By 19 I will forget to breathe only to be pumped back into reality

to be honest
Not all little girls plan a wedding before the age of twelve sometimes they plan funerals
Because it becomes easier to envision life from the sidelines than actually becoming the main character

Some little girls don't believe in fairytales, they believe in the crime scene and debauchery and chaos that is Greek and Roman mythology, so they become warriors or protectors or both shielding the fragrance of something fragile pressed into their palms by the gods that should be orchids instead of thorns

And sometimes, most times, these wars become as natural as breathing and they inhale the joy in embracing the blood and darkness hiding under their eyelids

And these girls, they play dress up too 'cause Greek goddesses were fashion moguls and their beauty became their only visible weapon and marriage, a business slaughterhouse tackling good judgment.

Dear Rudy Francisco,

If I had dreamt of my wedding at 12 I would not know of fate
Would still be so innocent, this vortex of stains would never bleed on me

I didn't dream of weddings, didn't care to know much except the color of my casket and
the number of pallbearers boiling flames from their throats

I dreamt of an open wound of feminism needed as sacred craters burning all who would draw the thin lines of manhood and protection into nuanced chivalry and abuse

If I dreamt of a wedding then I would not believe in fate
Would not know my church or song or dress would not dress my hair in the fashion I admired most
Or my nails, acrylics to scratch my last goodbye into the sky

And sometimes I think I have never thought of a wedding because I never thought of life as something worth living and I have never thought I'd make it to adulthood and if I should change a funeral plan to a wedding then hindsight says it may all be the same.

Dear Rudy Francisco,

I now imagine a train of vows so fast that the devil never sees when angels begin dripping from the lips of those who no longer marry suicide or homicide or both.

A letter to the smallest angels Earth never kept

Little One,
My deepest fear is seeing firsthand what it's like to lose a gift that was meant to last a lifetime.
I think those are scars that will never heal.
Those are fears that will never flee from the hearts of every parent.

Little One,
I'm trying not to cry as I go researching all that isn't right.
I'm trying to figure out how people become bartenders to grief.
I want to know where they learned to pretend as if surviving the impossible is not harder than it seems.
I want to meet the one who taught them that mourning meant adopting a blind spot for amnesia.
I want to see the first man to grieve without reminiscing.
I want to see how they came to the conclusion that getting through the days entailed denial of the fact that you no longer house air in your lungs, or how, like Thomas, they still doubt that the earth could break the order of things and digest something so small and so defenseless.

I wanted to know how death stares into the eyes of negotiating parents who offered their souls to save yours from the coldest embrace you will ever sleep in and still take you.
So I tried learning how many tearful screams it took to alter the joyous sounds of heaven's harps when a child sends its

soul packing from the world.

And the math wasn't what I hoped it would be.
So the first time I held you in my arms, I witnessed the resurrection of my deepest fears shape-shift into the nightmares of Beelzebub.

And I knew then that this reality had blinded me to seeing nothing but danger.
When you are in a position to ever lose something you begin to notice your pessimism worsen each time you quiet your subconscious to rely on angel numbers, knowing full well that it is impossible for the divine to congregate in the midst of the worldly.

And I still believe that the smallest caskets are the heaviest to carry.
Still believe that the tears that flow from each parent's eye are mirrored by the broken plans of the devil. How could death kiss the doors of innocent eyes before time?
How could God accept a dowry for a bride or groom who is still playing Double Dutch in sandboxes?

Dear Little One,
Because I can't tell what God has saved you from, I taught my heart to lift weights should I become a pallbearer to the horror story many parents dread
I wear the muscle of love on my sleeves should your innocence crumble underfoot
giving you unlimited access to the playground.

Shirley spoke of Little One,
I hope you know that the harder I work to hoard these tears
the quicker they fall.
So I imagine that the handlebars on your new chariot to
heaven have rusted for they once collected each droplet
from my eyes to make a necklace from my sadness and
keep you hydrated should you want for anything this world
has to offer.

And Little One, the windows must be blurry.

Little One, I cleared the Spanish needle that kept pricking
at your memory and replaced it with delicate flowers I had
for your dreams and your future. And I still find myself
struggling to keep my head above the water

Little One, when did love begin to hurt this way?
Do you know that I love you indefinitely, even though you
chose a definite end.

A letter to the sadistic bitch they call Poetry

I used to compare my love for you to August winds and streams of youth. Because in the past, I associated with people who watched open-heart surgeries in awe
As if it were the best sport ever created.

Before we met
I succumbed to peer pressure, forcing myself to listen to and bet on the hemorrhage of the brain in satisfaction, as if clogging my ears to the near death and discomfort of another would somehow lessen my own pain, and we told ourselves that this was empathic research so that we could lay claim to the stories these people hid beyond their smiles.

I thought that by taking all my darkness, you would cure my internal hatred.
I thought if you became my therapist, those days would be lost in a sea of forgetfulness. But the multiplication of these sins is what you seem to trigger in me.

I still find it hard to understand your methods, so tell me.
How does healing equate to gifting an audience misery injected from my marrow?
See, That's what standing on a stage does.
It challenges everything in you so that you can be successful, so that someone can listen to you and make you feel like your work isn't in vain.

But it has a trick to it.

All you have to do is let them know who you are.
Cut yourself under their light to prove you're human too.
Or pull your brains out.
Just so they can say that's some deep shit right there,
And I used to ask myself how that was possible.

So, Poetry, if you are the greatest healer of mind, spirit,
body, and soul, then tell me. How does forcing back anger
and tears pull at your heart strings? Tell me the words it
spoke to you.
Can you point out what part of my pain had you cracking
up with laughter? Tell me the parts that had goose bumps
forming on your arms.
Tell me how it is that you get off on my pain because maybe
Maybe then I'll know what story to share so you can finally
reach your climax.

You said I should open up and trust you.
I trusted you to read between the lines; instead, you saw
my story and applauded with snaps, continually screaming
out encore.

You didn't seem to care that I stood before you, naked and
broken. You only wished to reach out and tear me further.
so
I wonder how many of my stories you piled on top of each
other like bodies in a morgue, making confidential lists and
always writing when I open my mouth

I came for help, and you made me watch reruns of myself

frozen in time, suspended in the air, hanging from a thread and you held me for observation, whispering to me to trust that you would always have me.

So I did trust and I lay in your arms, where I learned to cry with my heart when the drought came for my eyes, and you held me until I fell asleep.

Poetry: if this was all to help me, then how did no one know that I woke up strapped to a bed? I was alive, but you wrote me up for death.
You had them do an autopsy on my still-warm body while you stole all my secrets and left me wide open for inspection.

I knew then that I couldn't trust you.

I knew then what it meant to be betrayed. And if this was all for profit, why did you claim that I could trust you?

I heard that you marketed the right to my voice, published my stories, and published papers on the narrations scraped from my throat. But you forgot one thing: it wouldn't be as deep as what was coming from my lips.

So you encouraged me with barbed whips, leaving my flesh stripped. Poison coursed through my veins, but my own venom refused to kill me.

So I was left standing alone. Naked, shivering, and lonely in front of your audience.

My drought long over.
For deep meant breaking down before everyone and reopening old wounds long forgotten. I guess it took me too long to realize that pain gets you off, and when you started snapping
I finally saw the beauty of my blood dripping from the heights of your fingers.

And I realize I am not the only one who is broken.

For the mended and complete never keep down the ones who still have to succeed.

So Poetry
I hope you finally get the help you need.

An ode to the house that built me

I've not learned how to let things go.
So, I still bottle my emotions; nobody must know.
I'm still young and haven't figured it all out, but I'm on a
journey to be the best version of myself,
whoever that might be.
And I wanted to make an apology for the place that's been
consistent in my misery. I'm sorry if I can't come
and face you.
The truth is, I'm not sure I know the way. That's a lie I tell
myself every day.

They keep saying no one will go back there.
As if it weren't where first steps were taken and memories
made. But no one wants the deed, and we all have various
reasons why the windows should be broken and blocks
removed from the surface. All while I'm silently thinking
that
If I walk through your halls again, I'll probably collapse.

I now know how to channel my emotions, but I haven't gone
back to the places where I've been hurt the most.
It seems as if those rooms come with cautionary measures
that I never saw, and the lady in the chair tells me I need
to find peace in the rooms I should have been safe in, so I
still peel police tape and homicide cards just to prove that
it's not the same walls that saw me caged.

I wish that it could still be my North Star, keeping me rooted and focused on making it in the world. I hear people talk about the places that grew them, and I'm worried that there is something deeply wrong with me if I hate the house that built me, but then I remember that there is nothing wrong with my heart; it's my brain that's at fault because it shields me from half the things I never saw and the things I did see, leaving me cut off from having ties to the place like Black people born in a land they built but told to go back to one they have no recollection of, but I'm still telling myself that I'm different because

I still remember the walls that cornered me in.

The pale yellow that should have been like sunshine on cold, dark days didn't seem so refreshing when you lay there, hearing the pounding of your heart over the hum of mosquitoes.

And I remember laying still as if I were playing possum and trying to challenge those with no life in their lungs because I didn't have much fight left in me, just freeze or fawn, and I froze for years in a panicked haze, waiting for the jaws of life to pull me out, but I never fully awoke. I remember becoming zombified and doing as told because "children obey your parents" was all I could hear, and I folded me in a box to be shipped to the afterlife until I had use for her again, and that's when I fawned.

I think I played the first chair to Ageon's song of Fire and Ice, pretending everything was alright because I was told it was, but I never found the courage to build citadels from broken hearts, and they say that if you hear the gunshot, then it probably wasn't meant for you. I just can't remember if I heard the bangs or not, and I can't remember if the broken heart syndrome is caused by knowing safe isn't safe, and I don't know if I should call myself a waif, a vagabond, or a nomad.

And it's creepy how many places I've laid my head since leaving where I don't fit.

I haven't yet quenched this homesick thirst, stayed overhydrated, and waged war with my electrolytes because I don't want to be thirsty for home. And maybe it's because I have yet to abate the guilt.
I've regressed while moving forward, blaming the house for the monster as if concrete walls could birth sheep in wolf clothing and not angels. Maybe no matter how long I've left home, I'll still remember where I came from and the scandal I left behind for others to glean.

No matter how far I chase the lightning from the skies or my shadows from my feet, I can't hypnotize Chrysaeon into wiping those days away. I have no recollection of becoming the simpleton these children learn of, but I learned to be a jockey to deter the mistakes I made, pelting hubris into the ground should I make a spectacle of myself, and I hate that this world cares for no one. I hate that the quicksand I keep skipping over is handcuffed to my ankles.

And I can't pray to God without zoning off and wondering

what
I'm talking about in the moment, so maybe one day, when
half the neighbors don't blame me for the sins the house
collapsed in, I can rent the place as an escape house and
make it home again.

Dear the house that built me, it's not your fault
I never learned to be resilient.

In memo-rum of the peers who never chose to stay past 22

I heard that the bell knelled twice this year to draw each person to the viewing of
Closed doors on the friends whose faces were dismantled.

It seems like these bad days have a tendency to blend into each other. And it's scary to think about how they felt, drawing their last breath and bracing for the impact of the unknown on what happens after death. I don't believe that angels exist, but I still hope that they made it to the celestial chambers.

Call it wishful thinking and daydreaming, but I keep praying for their souls as if repentance could enter the grave. I hope they had time to claim him. I'm missing two peers from my childhood, but somewhere there are siblings and best friends—parents, grandparents, spouses, cousins, uncles, and aunts —who have left half their hearts buried in the woods beneath the churches that christened them.

I don't remember a time I have ever been scared of death. Now it's like a house of cards, and the wind keeps whispering that all bad things come in threes, so with a knot in my chest, I find myself distracted from my thoughts and somehow still asking God who will be next. I don't think I've ever cried this hard, and I'm afraid to be 22 going on 23 because I'm in the death zone and freak accidents and unexplained situations can happen.

I want to control my destiny, but how does that happen?

When I believed that seven was a lucky number, a Biblical figure, and seven is the number that tore a few hearts that will never heal, I guess the day of love wasn't enough to stop the flow of magazines.

I thought I'd be over my fear of vehicles, but when they ask, "do you plan to ever get back behind the wheel?" I begin to hyperventilate as I imagine how you felt with a rebar stuck through your torso prematurely stopping the pulsating heart in your stomach. I know you must have clutched it to protect the child being torn from you. You were a mother who never saw the face of your child, but you must have felt his heartbeat stop, and I don't know if that's when you gave up the fight and died.

But I'm being told that I can't hide from the world and have a life free of depression and fear.

I've got to remember to breathe and see that our few memories and conversations are treasured and transformed into the best of my life. I've got a picture I still look at.
The picture I have has half of us missing, but the angels are still there.

Funny how that felt like a lifetime ago. When we all thought we had so much time left. You both taught me that life is short.
But it's not a lesson I like because bonds never seem to die

with distance, time, or strife.

I guess I'll always miss you when I remember your smile, and I'll always cry when I remember the talents you never got to share with a class of children calling you by your name. I hope heaven has a choir because your voice was impeccable.

That's the thing I hate the most about death: that when you're gone, you'll always be on my mind.

Isn't it funny we never found the time to talk more than a couple minutes every other month, and my pride took all the joy in linking up.

Guess I thought you'd look at me weird after you told me what you knew. I loved that I made you know how I felt about you, and I guess that's why you hit the hardest, because who will mock the school you took pride in? You might have never walked down that graduation aisle, but you're still a teacher to me because I'm still learning the value of not caring what anyone else may think.

Now it's like I'd sell the days to the highest bidder just to make one last memory, just to see you walk down the second form block and smile when you hail me, because your smile after that serious face was worth it. I'm sorry for all who never saw it.

I hate that I now have time to think of you because it's too late to make a difference in a bond that time tried to weaken.

Fly high, my angels. Mother's Day and Valentine's Day will never be the same for the rest of us that remain. I promise we'll all find a way to make life worth living and stay in touch, because if there's one thing I've learned, it's that life is short and efforts are timeless.

Long live the two whose memories won't ever fade from the hearts of Beaulah's 1994-2004 Youths, may you fly higher than the highest eagles and keep each other company.

Not a bildungsroman, but one day

Hey Black girl, don't you know you're beautiful? Hey Black girl, don't you know it's fun to be alive? Hey Black girl, you're almost an adult now.

You're almost at the age where you won't need to gag on respect for the elderly, who make you feel belittled because you're afraid of stepping on toes and disgracing those who raised you.
Adulthood means releasing your tongue from the hold you have on it. It means stepping out.
It means being as loud as you possibly can.
It means telling your mind without consequence to the feared or favored. It means being responsible and not making excuses for your actions and downfalls.

Hey Black girl! I can't wait until I can see the sunlight beaming from your windowsill, but we've got five years to go before you learn to dance to the tunes in your head.

Hey Black girl, promise me that you won't ever lose your smile.

Hey Black woman, I look into your eyes sometimes to see them coughing up pain
And I think that maybe it's better to not have grown up at all if all I have to look forward to are empty days in bed. I think about the light from the outside, and my mind bleeds in agony, so I feign sickness and press snooze twenty times

each morning. I think if the rapture comes, I may miss it if I'm not careful.

Black woman, I stare into your face, and I no longer see the Black girl with a golden future but a new identity of doom stitched into the printed insoles of your feet.

Dear Black woman, I wonder if you know your destiny doesn't have to change with your mood.
I wonder if they ever think of you as a hermit for not having the energy to leave those cold rooms.

Black woman I wish you knew that depression was a form of gas. I wish you knew that this mate of yours would make it impossible to eat, bathe, or sleep.

Dear Black woman, did you know that your favorite color would devour you?
Leave your leftovers for dogs like the sores of Lazarus before gates that won't accept you.

Dear Black woman, I wish you could cloak yourself in the skin of another so that you could experience all you have to offer.

Dear Black woman, did the Bible not tell you that you need the innocence of a child to see you through?
Do you not know that prayer works miracles?

Dear Black woman, why have you pawned the tongue that

anchors your faith in Pandora's box of lies?

Dear Black woman, you've got the strength to break free. I'm trying to believe in you.

Hey! Black woman! Do you know that you're still beautiful, not only when you dress to fit the part?
Hey! Black woman! Don't you know it's still fun to be alive? It's a real testimony.
Hey! Black woman! You're an adult now, and with bookmarked chapters of your life, you don't have to keep reading.
Hey! Black woman! Cough the pain out, and embrace your destiny because with God all things are possible.

Dear Black woman, why won't you just trust Him and lean on Him? Dear Black woman, His yolk is easy, so you will never have to worry about being someone else's burden.

Unaddressed letters

I saved my suicide notes
buried them beneath the crucible of my soul
mounded them into the reaper's anthills
and embraced the times I've wanted to die.

The four times I've attempted to give God a helping hand,
but he refused to take the breath I borrowed. I heard that
we all had a choice.
Our lives were our own to do what we wanted with them,
and it's funny how I'm still alive.

I guess God himself didn't want me, but I can't really blame
him. I read my suicide letters with tears creeping through
my pores. And I felt alive enough to feel something.
Alive enough to burn it with the tip of a cigarette.
And I promised myself, while burning flesh and paper at
that moment, that I'd stop smoking. I lit lavender and vanilla
candles and watched them burn in silence.
Reverencing the death of thoughts soon forgotten.
Well enough to count the constellations, naming scars like
broken teardrops.

In that moment, I whispered that
This is no longer for whoever finds me dead
It's for those who find me alive today and living.
And I vowed to live on Doomsday.
The wretched day I came into this world, every night at half
past twelve, I fly awake.

Tangled in sheets mingled with sweat and broken crystals. I've heard that I don't sleep well at night because I've got too much on my mind. I know I don't sleep well at night because the cancer of my past pecks my flesh for bread.

I've broken families that broke me, and I'm guilty of dividing a house. I had no right to speak about things that were private.
Now the word sorry bitterly combs through the spaces of teeth and tongue
A word encapsulated within the creased bookmarks of a broken life
Suffocating dream demons and keeping nightmares alive
I've learned to fight in my sleep. Just to be beaten by life.

I've saved my suicide notes, but I'm still practicing death more times than I've given thanks for life and held onto the power to horde pain and keep myself behind.
So believe me when I say I know the voice enough to know that it's not truthful but not enough to discard it.

I know that we sometimes can't let go of the feeling that this is not enough and that it can cost you everything and nothing at all. It becomes this lingering cloud between you that sits cold and heavy on your chest and won't allow you to move on,
and I know no one truly moves on; we just learn to live with it and try healing and shutting the voice down, but it comes back every time. Believe me when I say that this isn't the last of the fight, and it may not even be the hardest you'll

face, but the people you ultimately leave behind,
I hear, are the ones who will suffer most.

So, if today is the day you've had enough, then hold onto
the lifeline of my voice because I've been through the fire
and I'm still walking through this thick smoke just to make
it to the other side.

I wrote a suicide note and wished that somewhere in
another life I am normal again
and I pray every night that all this fighting to survive, was
not a waste as it seems.
And I wake up believing each morning that fearing survival
is only one way of making it out alive, then I ask myself
what's next?

Dear Mr. Right Now

Baby, you showed up in my nightmares again.

Your throat slit from side to side, and your head rolling from the guillotine. And somehow, you survived like
Mary Webster.
And you took to braiding Loretta's silver thread and golden needle into tassels, as if you won lotteries worth celebrating.

My Love, the quicksand in your arms took me in like I needed adopting, and I became your avatar, fighting wind, fire, and the other one. Calculating algorithms to make you my Barack
But little did I know that leg irons shackled me to Harlem nights, with no manual for the lonely nights telling me I could never be your Mitchell.

See, I wanted a love with the simplicity and innocence of Synclaire and Obby mixed with the allure of Blanche and Regine and the spice of Kyle and the Maverick.
But
These cheat codes have doused my home with the dark liquor and whiskey your white liver left at my door. And I thought the mat said this was a drama-free zone. This was a happy home.

Did you know that before you, my nightmares had Ol' Higue? I was surprised to see you in her counsel, like a rolling calf. I thought I would see you in my dreams with the butterflies my stomach no longer held.

But Baby

You showed up in my nightmares again, and made me wish
the earth was flat
so that I could drive to the edge and sit, watching the whites
of your eyes turn over, as you sleep in the vineyards, ready
for the harvest of pain and suffering.
But I remember that even as rigor mortis set in, you could
be heard telling me you loved me still. That you'd walk the
provincial gardens of the afterlife with me.

I had it all wrong.

Baby, I think my body is trying to tell me something I don't
want to hear. The prophets told me you'd keep showing
up in my nightmares until I can understand how to put
myself first. Until I no longer garnish my fingers with your
rings and I can open the mouth of my heart to receive me
without throwing up.

See, I'd step on steel or plunder for you, My Love.
Watch with dumb stoicism until your face isn't the one
pelting me with the phobias.
I confided in you.
I guess I love you too much to see the scandal you've made
of me.
I guess it's true what they say.
Sometimes all you need for satisfaction is to sit silent and

watch the day fly by, and maybe then Eros will give me the right one.

I still hope you're the right one.

For my childhood friend B.A.D.

I've got friends who move like family, but there is one I never truly thanked.

A friend who stuck around from childhood holding on to the definition of success that has led me on a path less traditional to the route I want.

So for the friend who used pep talk and support, like the vices of crashing tornados against galless plans for the future, the friend who wormed her way like harmless sepsis into my frontal lobe.

The friend I have nothing in common with but communication issues. And I thank God on occasion for this fixture of human life holding me accountable while I hold secrets dear.

Though I never say it often, I love you deeply, and I'm always so grateful for the times you thought to pour into me.

So forgive me for never trusting you enough to see me the same. Forgive me for walking away without a heads up.

I get that running is in my nature.

Forgive me for reshuffling the meaning of childhood, a period of lifespan between infancy and adolescence.

Forgive me for letting the distance get so far that I sometimes feel like I can never recoup the train.

But I am still here, wishing you all the great things this world has to offer and checking up on you, although I should do it more often, because you had a hand in aiding parts of me that matter.

And that is my confidence, outlook, fashion, and questioning the norms and morals we were told we should follow.

And for that, I will always be indebted.

A letter I never sent will never send

~~Dear K.O.H~~
~~Dear brother~~
To whom it may concern,

They say that sometimes, no matter how hard or how far
you push some people, they will still jaywalk their way back
into the fire that is your company.
They will tear apart a piece of themselves and sew it onto
your heart to prove you are one and the same—no blood
involved.
Will carousel you into forgetting that you fear abandonment,
and the definition reminded me of my brother, whose
resilience was anything short of annoying.

~~Dear brother,~~

Sometimes I forget that you are not only the blueprint for
success but so much more human than a sibling.
Or child, or friend.
Sometimes, when you take the world into your hands so
that we cannot identify it, I forget that you were never apart
of the constellations, just the placeholder of a star through
every sky we walk under, so nothing ever falls on us. On
me mostly. And you became the male version of Soteria.

And maybe it's all because you coddled me like your love
didn't need discouragement from all my faults and quietness
and I'm scared for you, because every time I push you away,

you boomerang back with a piece of the past and who I was strapped across your back, like you're trying to remind yourself that I am worth the trouble of bringing with you.

And maybe that's all wishful thinking on your part, because I'm not worth all the trouble. If I'm worth anything at all.
And maybe our faith is already written, and we will never be as close as we were when we were children.
And I never apologized for tearing through a bond made in the womb. Never gave reason for walking away and going mute.
And I couldn't hold you back, from the purpose I knew you had, so I never told you to stay. I said I'd follow behind and created confusion instead of memories, love, and friendship, and hoped you'd be frustrated enough to have the sense to walk away.

~~Dear brother,~~

Why did you never walk away, and in every poem that I write, I start leaving a part of me that you may find? Sometimes all I leave between pages is a fear I never showed, or the courage I no longer own.

~~Dear brother,~~

I cannot disown this minefield, still clinging to my shadow, reminding me of how explosive I am when I stay in my head too long.
How paranoid and defensive every whisper and joke

makes me.

How every secret leaves the house and returns to the same room at 1 a.m. every day or every second Friday.

Alcoholism was never the vice that lived among us,

Sometimes I wonder how many of us held secrets we still hoard. And I suppose this is what it means to honor a family that has already fallen without getting too messy.

Without gathering enough evidence to overdose on memories.

I am too stubborn to be called a victim before daughter.

To be called a daughter before an individual, too humble not to point out that I no longer associate with anything, but not too prideful to shut down and bulldoze myself from all lives.

Dear brother,

I left my lifeline buried in the palm of your hands the day my heart ran out of my eyes. I tore my fists from their sides to make the picture perfect, or make the pencil worth its time. The paper worth her sacrifice.

And in all the chains I used, you never could understand the message inside.

I wish you had stopped to watch the pages bleed instead of holding the sky so I wouldn't ever be hurt because I already was.

Dear K.O.H.,

I still wish I believed that you understood, and maybe one day we'll find our way back to that bond.

But that's just wishful thinking, because that's impossible when I keep pushing to be lonely and alone, for that's the best place I have ever found a comfortable home.
but I pray you know I love you too.

Dear Woman

I've practiced death more times than I've given thanks for
life. Swallowed hatred and breathed circles of misplaced
anger and regret through the pores of so many scars—it's
like I'm living a lie.
and nothing in life tends to make much sense
Except that my multitude of sighs is a thunderous roar still
equipped to shake the throne of God

CHAPTER IX
Amour

"How does one collect love, rage, hatred, fear...?"

~ James Reece

I can't build my home in you

[28]See my heart, my heart ain't been broken.

Still can't find a body I can build my home in, but I'm still searching between the bed sheets of the broken for a place I can watch the sunsets of Heaven, but boy you ain't worth it when we both wash our secrets in necromancy seducing demons and you can bring me to the edge of the river but deep down as much as I want it I know you can never be the chosen

You can't even be the land I build my home on yet
I can still hear how your grating lust transforms into a youthful tapestry of bloodshed and I know your body ain't worth the haunting, but your body, boy your body ain't have no reason looking this damn good when sickness lives within its reach, watering down my ambitions when I try to pluck your weeds.
See, I can't build my home in you 'cause your grandfather, your grandfather's ghost still follows you, teaching you and my great grandmother's family values ain't been passed onto me.

So, I don't know how to Christmas-wrap your sins and call them holy.
See, I hold grudges instead of forgiveness, treasure bitterness before I do friendships or lovers. My method's selfish. And my love ain't know her own faults, but she's both judge and executioner.

---

28 *"Love is like the rain. It comes in a drizzle sometimes. Then it starts pouring and if you're not careful it will drown you." ~ Edwidge Danticat, Breath, Eyes, Memory*

Boy you can't stand trial here, can't let the sun smile on you in my sheets 'cause I can't be trusted to keep my heart whole when you're around.

And my heart ain't been broken until she looked in the mirror searching for battle scars to match your story, and she wonders why you would leave your grandfather's infidelity tracking a muck through my living room.

So, boy you can't sleep here no more 'cause I still ain't learnt my great grandmother's tolerance and I ain't the patient woman. Oftentimes I won't see past certain misunderstandings. I'm not comfortable in dirt so I can't be your homemaker, but I'm still searching for my home in someone I can dance with when the sun comes up.

Boy I can't be your curtain call secret 'cause see, my body, my body still ain't been touched right ain't felt heat trespass like sin in so long. She still craves your dominance and your words, your words still fill my stomach like a five course meal, but boy, you're someone else's home, yet it's scary how much I crave the merging of these two mutilated beings like an obsession only God can curb.

Baby boy I can't curb you but I can't build a home in you either, and isn't this just all reckless? Just another fatal attraction bound to leave my heart a wrangled mess and my heart, my heart ain't never been broken before but by loving you she is starting to learn what hurt is.

Boy I want to borne you nations

Push forth twelve tribes to give your name to I want to raise
you up like Mansa Musa Boy, I want to make you billions,
build you citadels from the ashes of the fallen, make you
my modern day Abraham
I want to laugh at promises and give you both legacy and
triumph boy I want to be the answer to your prayers want
to be your stone to kill your Goliaths boy I want to suck you
in like communion wine

want to braid your hair and share your throne
I want to love you like you're the only man deserving of
grace and I'm not really asking for a lot, not trying to live
in your face

I'm not the clingy type but I want to fester on your heart
like a sore you can't shake, curl up inside your spine so with
the pressure you don't break
Want to grind success into your super baby I want to savor
the Divineness you offer from your plate want the peace
and the H.E.A [29]the smile that never fades

I want to be both nature and nurture boy I want to be your
safe place the rub your scalp and cradle your head on my
lap Netflix and chill date
I don't need the Cinderella story that's too basic
Don't want the Bonnie and Clyde love that seems to end
quick and seven Spanish angels just ain't my luck I don't
want to live inside your

29 *happily never after*

skin I want to be engraved onto your genome, boy I want to be the only ink illustrated on your bones, I want the promise of forever, twin flames that burn eternal, soul ties that won't unbind

Boy I need a worship type of love, the one protected by the vows of the spirit above
So
Baby if you truly are the rib of my rib, then I want to live inside your skin like I'm the hypodermis protecting your organs
I want the marriage
and the romance vows in the midst of praise and worship cause heaven coming down upon this union may be the only way to establish survival

I want to be the air that threatens your lungs when you forget to think of me see, baby I don't really require much but I still believe in romance don't like optimistic fairy tales but I still crave masquerade balls and a slow waltz so when you come knocking at the doors to my heart remember I'm not the girl who believes in the simplicity of love but somehow I love hard and I contradict myself a lot
but I don't want to bury a love fated to die so if this ain't meant to be then I'll wait for the level of trust we create.

I opened Pandora's box

to show him why I keep this pantry of boundaries close
brought forth remnants of decomposed tear ducts and cut
knuckles from the flowerbeds I still toil, placed them at an
altar with this ring of purity and said "Lord consume this
misunderstood paradox that I have become before I stand
here with someone not worthy of my love, take this crippled
cornerstone and make it master peace"
'cause it sounds so easy but never really is when you're
the culprit misguidedly issuing excuses to excuse your
exertions from saying no to every advance

told him 99 percent won't cut it
'cause when you settle for the bare minimum you
involuntarily enable habitual beacons of low priorities and
selfishness and that value just almost always seems to
depreciate

See I will always have a table that needs no helper and I
hope he has one too so our linked goals can sit together
or at least be neighbors
I call this merging of resources generational wealth for our
children and not generational trauma call it hope for our
future

See, I'm still working on myself
Still climbing the mountains I'm stretching past five foot
three to see
see, I believe in checking all boxes

call me obsessive but routine is in my marrows, it's some sort of compulsion my hard NO(s) will always stay rooted in my mind and actions

Yes I'm mule-headed and stubborn so ain't no changing that I've got priorities aligned with purpose and God
and anyone worthy of my time better have some ambition compelling him to reign in his vices
and I'm hoping one day when he sends me that 100% he would already have ejaculated all his triggers into communication and not promiscuity because unless he does the work then my doors are closed
'cause everyone seems to be God-sent, some just never seem to have the right address

Worth it

Truth be told I'm just disappointed that I can't seem
to trust you
Washed you from my mind but you're still
imprinted on my soul
'Cause once upon a time I burnt sage for you
Put my body through the purge to satisfy yours
Spilt-roasted my emotions so you wouldn't feel hurt 'cause
Boy if I'm being honest I would have died for you
Topanga to your Corey I would have aligned my choices to
spend more time with you
Now even when my feet adapt the speed of flow Jo like
Maxine Shaw I won't chase after you
'Cause every time I did I'm left hurt by a nigga who couldn't
see love through

See so many niggas tore me apart just to water him, now
I'm searching for someone who starts out loving me ten
times more than I do them
So if I got to drop my standards like Gina I'll find a Martin
at the altar
In the end certain fables prove right and duty always win

But I'm still searching for the day justice puts some luck in
our stars like the letters spell eternity
Sprinkle a little reality in this twilight classics be damned
and boy forgiveness ain't worth it if all dogs really go to
heaven 'cause if two can play this game then I'll mirror that
white girl circling the blocks

Baby I can be a bitch in demand so boy don't play with my heart when she's not in command of my mind
I'm irrational and impulsive hot pressed together to make life chaotic

The Pink to your Fonzie you don't stand a chance if you break me my pen moves faster than the speed of light baby I'll have you in a panic

but really truth be told I'm just disappointed I can't seem to trust you

after all that I gave you, you still choose to toss me like we were Shawn and Angela doomed from the start and I'm pretty sure love doesn't measure up to reality when emotions toe the line not leaving enough time to mend things bitten into just ask Klaus and Caroline

But maybe someday I'll get over this and end up right where we started taking notes from Professor Wayne and Whitley on engineering the perfect strategies to fight for someone worth it baby I pray we're worth it

The catcalling man on the street said "smile girl"

as if saying
Let me give you something to be thankful for girl

And I want to cut these lips and gift wrap it's smoldering
curls for him since he likes it so much,
Let it's lightning ignite a bubbling in the acid of his stomach
become the reflux that ultimately destroys the manhood
he holds dear

See, a man's own enemy is his pleasure
The man on the street said "smile more"
I want to say that this asymptote be a choked gasped
Be an ancient relic of mischief situated in a museum of
terror curating curves that dance to a music of their own
making

My smile is the hollow gates into Dante's inferno
A deathtrap coiled into Victorian pleasure houses meant
to break the camel's back
An epileptic artichoke that cannot be peeled
It is written that my smile is the silver still feared by wolves
A shooting comet pulsating past every ecliptic moon
A seance separating the covering of bones

The man on the street said I should learn to smile more
Pity that he doesn't know that even the devil takes notes
when the diabolical edges of my teeth break free for air
My smile is the overlooked front matter of a book

The hard case that makes a G18 better death than sulfur
dioxide
My smile be the lion's den only God has the ability to close
once open
The man on the street said "smile girl" and I watch the
compost of his life pour over the concrete words I stuff back
Down his throat like why smile...

just because you tell me to

When he said that he only dates suicidal women because they have nothing to lose

He sounded like a disillusioned Gen-Z kingpin calling Pizza Hut to order a side of murder with his meal without knowing what he was getting himself into
So I tested his limit, fondled the theory of loving someone whose expiration date was in the eye of any mistake or bad day
Then, I stared him in the eye and placed the gun on my temple, rolled the chamber back and pulled, and I never flinched.

But he screamed how insane I was when he realized that the bullet never went off.
I said this is the never-ending game we will play when you have my heart.
You will pull once at me and then at you, and whoever is without a pulse first wins.
Because if he cannot go headfirst into danger with me, then he cannot possibly know how it feels to want to die but not have the courage to do it yourself.

He cannot know how it feels to stand still, welcome death into our hearts like she is a god worth loving
Will never be able to hide little Sara in his closet and wear her corpse as accessory on occasion
He does not know how it feels to stand in the gap for someone who has no intention of staying for 6:23 when the chapter finally closes.

He said he only dated suicidal women,
And I found out that it was for show because when he saw
me dying, he rescued me
And maybe he had a hero complex or maybe he loved to
feel needed and he thinks that it is an honorary thing to
save someone who wishes to be dead.

He thinks that it makes my life easier to know that he grew
attached to where death could hurt him.
And he said he no longer dates suicidal women,
Said he could never get used to pulling muskets from thin
air just to swallow what is left of love rouletted to stop
breathing.

I said the one shot left was mine, so he braced himself for
the impact of impulsiveness that never came.
And I made the idea of loving him die, because I was too
accustomed to planting myself in the throes of danger
And never once have I needed saving on this odyssey to
death.

To the man who used my love as a less-than-average footnote

Thank you
because now I know why Mama said I seduced daimons,
said I have ever since she bled me to what should have been
death said even drowning, I could love the wrong out of
anyone, as if bleeding them to be halal
Mama said that I no longer see anything
but nature but society
and Mama ain't never been wrong
so thank you for making me see how impertinent my love
was

If my heart could speak

Did you know that I tried to reprint my heart and stuff it back between my sternum?
[30]Do you know I do this to keep her from ever abandoning me?
And I tell her it is to keep her safe from armor-piercing bullets that I never learned of.
Do you know that sometimes my heart becomes a morse code just so she can whisper to me?
Sometimes she tells me that every little victory is worth celebrating because I am still breathing.

But
If my heart could speak, it would tell you about all the times I've broken it. It would tell you that I'm selfish, and I would drown myself in liquid fire just to prove that I can
If my heart could speak, she would say that I've tried convincing her that I'm right for breaking away from people because I'm afraid they will see that I'm not worth it and leave.
So I leave first and never look back because I tell myself that the distance is better in the long run.

If my heart could speak
She would say that I ignored her.
She would say that I think my mind is always right.
Say that she has watched me lumberjack her roots twice, so when I said that I wasn't trying to die by the pills, it was probably an eighth of the truth. But if my heart could

---

30 Oscar Wilde famously said that the heart was meant to be broken. In circumstances where this isn't true, I've realized that the heart must first be broken into in order for anything of substance to take root and subsequently grow there.

scold, she would reprimand me for the harm I've done her all these years.

If my heart could walk
She would put on her dancing shoes and sashay out the door, like so many before her.
So to keep her from drinking poisoned syndromes from Stockholm glasses, I'm trying to find a way to convince her that I don't hate the ones who tried to help me. I just hate myself for being weak and needing help.

If my heart could speak
She would ask me if all this was worth it. So before she does I'm struggling just to find meaning in the process because how do you know when you've healed if all you do is repaint the destruction of your purpose? When all you do is see the eyes of pity and scrutiny as if you are still stuck in the cement around your torso?

So excuse me if I say that I understand euthanasia.
If I say that, I applaud those who got away because they were courageous and unselfish enough to try.

Excuse me if my heart remains shattered under the bulletproof vest I wear to keep me safe.

Do you know that if my heart could speak, she would pray for the voice of the gods and scream to the mountains that she is proud of me?

Do you know that sometimes when this world is quiet, I hear the roar of my heart as she shouts Igbo and Yoruba cries of war for me?

Do you know my heart is a Congolese drum, that lingers far from its rightful continent but she still beats when all else is silent?

Did I tell you that my heart could speak?

Obituaries for love

Someone once asked me
"How is it that you love with faith?"
Said "how do you know when it's time to give up on
something that's no longer worth it?" She said that when
love goes cold,
Can you ever blow life back into its frail lungs?

She asked how I learned to love you. And how well did it
end?

I toiled with the question.
Looked her in the eyes and responded that although they
taught us
Dead bodies were only found in cemeteries, they regretted
mentioning
scorched kisses from men whose broken-barreled guns
lay discarded by the white outlines of shapely corpses
long forgotten. Corpses whose last breath resonates like
a recurring echo of depravity in the minds of the damned.
Whose screams of betrayal howl at Levites with bloody
hands?
Levites whose eyes will not meet those of writhing souls
Still hanging onto hope that this is all a joke and nothing
beautiful has the audacity to end this sad

I told her

They never told us that before they killed us, our brethren

would search beneath our bosoms, to see how far we could push love, for they had the keys to the bars God placed on our hearts
And
We called them our knights in shining armor.

But these were men who sharpened their swords on our knives like broken floorboards.
Men who picked their teeth on the bones of our cages to teach us we were worthless.
Men who taught us that the things we wanted were what they whispered Trump-In-g decolonization by telling us that the only place we belong is on our knees men who spat on our scriptures as we lapped at roots between their thighs.

I said,
I loved him.
I loved him more than I would ever have loved myself, and I guess that's the sin in me speaking
because
How can I love someone?
who discarded my most fragile pieces, like excess parts of puzzle manuals not worth reading.

See,
I've always believed we were tainted for too long by the carcasses of dead men calling themselves warriors.
And even then,
We searched the pages of obituaries, like dating sites.

We used hearses as shopping carts as we built the perfect foundation to conceal the cracks in the chest plates of men we could fix.

I told her that
When love dies, our first instinct is to return his scars. Or, better yet, thank God for promises left unfulfilled. But I've come to realize that time doesn't heal all wounds. Some we wear as badges of honor,
and some we hide beneath the cupboards of bathroom sinks, but we have all loved someone more than we loved ourselves.

Women have all somehow learned the art of giving themselves as plastic Barbies in case they suffer from phimosis.

So,
We've all been veterans of war, too worn to recall past events.
We've all watched sin bobbing in the throats of prideful men who have betrayed us because they find it hard to swallow their shame. So, somehow, they pass it on to the next of kin. I wonder if he knows that we know that his Adam's apple is only a secret lodged in places our eyes can't physically see.

I told her that sometimes love has to die for us to realize it was only lust dressed as infatuation. And it's hard when you finally realize that, those love stories that are buried are never really worth the memory.

When a boy speaks

I see the desire falling from the crown of his head as pretty
becomes more than my mama's shallow compliment, and I
am left hoping that this one takes no well
because the ring on my finger is promise-made purity
welded into stainless steel,
and that's enough repellent for his kind
is enough grenade pin to make him think again about his
approach to sweet nothings that I laugh and blush at while
refusing to give him my name. Give him my number.
my time
and he thinks he is getting somewhere by telling me that I
am sweetness defined.
that I have a face that could steal any man's heart and crush
the sole of his dreams with a singular smile.
I tell him that even if he should have the power to breech
me into liking him,
He does not have the strength to make me stay. To anoint
our union into one and sign away the rights to myself for
his utmost pleasure.
and no one has ever gotten close enough for me to see
myself in violation of contracts I made with God to wait for
the person who could replace the ring on my finger with
another promise of forever.
So I keep vigils for these boys as they come, hoping to find
another conquest in me.
I say hymns for the time they have killed in gaining nothing.
and whisper that this synagogue cannot brandish itself as
a tally on their tongue.

cannot Christopher Columbus its way into small black
books until the purity is washed in marriage.
is washed in holiness is witnessed by God.
Becomes I do without takeback

Let me go

I read my horoscope today. It said I'd have peace in abundance, but every time I close my eyes
I see you smiling from my canthal region and I don't know what to do with your existence in my life anymore than I know what to do with the tears at my feet but I saw a love bump and thought you were thinking of me. Then I remembered how you doxxed me.
and I wasn't sure if you'd be recyclable or not.
So I left you sitting at my dining table, contemplating the thunder in my words and the wind that tore our house like Samson and the Philistine temple
And then
I hated that I loved you so much.
I hated that I wanted you to come sweep me off my feet, baby I don't like how our love is beginning to feel like a suicidal plunge into Lover's Leap.
I don't like the constant betrayal and barely talking.
But each time you grip my thighs, I am left believing that this is what I want. That the makeup is so much better than the peace my heart so desperately sought, and I know it's wrong to stay, but I can't leave you this way.
So do me a favor and be gone for me before you break me any other way. Baby.
Can I just have some peace?
I don't want to get used to this type of pain because
There's nothing more pitiful than a woman with nowhere to run and nothing to gain from a love gone bad.

Break my heart

I thought about writing a love poem. and I'm not the type to
but I wanted to see the eclipse in your eyes resemble mine.
wanted to switch the x and y axis so that I could alternate
between safe and secure. because if your love was real then
I wouldn't be left waiting for scraps at your feet.
I guess you don't truly see the real me.
the vulnerable side of need in my nakedness and I'm trying
hard to fix myself. so that I don't go wishing gloom on
another pagan holiday.
baby
I want a love so pure that I'm forced to believe in the naiveté
that is Valentine's Day. and
If your love was real,
I would still be drinking from the cocktail of your eyes and
swimming in rose petals hidden deep in the recesses of
your mind.
I wonder how we ever got to the point of no return? Baby,
I really want to know.
It's like we're enticing each other by melting gold to wash
betrayal away. As if money equates to love
See
I want a love that doesn't make me wonder.
I want a love that gives me the hands of Iaso. because
I want to heal a broken heart like I do a broken limb.
and I want to fight to keep you near me.
But
I haven't gotten the hang of breakups yet. so
I think I may die from the depth I have to fall. because I was

so in love with you. and you had me so goddamn confused. had

My heart throbbing. hand shaking morning sickness and the latest of awkwardness

That's how much I love you every day.

and I don't know how I'll ever be this gullible again. So, dear future husband

I may not deserve your love when you come. I may not wait by your side in servitude.

I may not even dote on you.

But I'll pray for this bitterness to go away. I pray that God opens my heart to your wonders. and all you have to offer

I just hope you're patient enough to stay with a woman who may ruin you, though she doesn't mean to And like Angelica Schuyler I wish you satisfaction

Grown folk secrets

He sprayed baygon at me and said, "Damn mama.

F**k with me, and you'll see the type of princess turned queen you'll be. Now, if you let me

I can run my hands through the waves north of your thighs. and break the headboards with your tie-head on,"

And normally I wouldn't answer catcalls.

but I wanted to see if this was all bark and no bite. So I let him speak his shit.

He said,

"I want to see how glazed your eyes get when I rapture in your gut.

and each wisp of my emotion is fused to the lips playing peek-a-boo with your blue tea."

He said,
"Baby, let me baptize you in the immaculate conception of
my sins. Roughly pin you down in tag and spread you on
the counter pane to lay the pipes you thought were broken."
He said he would make a hallmark of my beauty.

So I asked him to capture Polaroid images of how I drank
in each touch from him, like it was red Kool-Aids at Black
barbecues. As if our lips don't have enough nectar to put
bees out of business.
and every kiss from him has me thinking I'm loyal to the end.

Like Bonnie never left Clyde when she had the audacity to
die, and Thelma wasn't ever sick of Louise.
He grabbed my throat and said he knew how much I liked
to act like a jackrabbit, and that's just the freak in me.

So he treats me like a slut, but he wants a girl who can
switch it up.
a girl who can do it in the backseat but chooses to have her
back blown out by rims. uncomfortable enough to make
love the punchline of desire.

He said he loved the soft part of me.
That turns black and blue with every new bruise he puts
on me
That I relax him, keep him calm and centered, and I wouldn't
jinx him. He said he knows where home is.
And I know how to behave like a good girl when I'm reminded
of my place in his world

as if I'm not choosing to look past how he acts on these streets. As if I'm not sanctimonious enough not to hit back I guess

Baby Boy doesn't know that I know that he gets around. but I'm not invested in this, so I let him be. 'Cause we ain't hiding, but we're private.

handling grown people's business and communicating. because

It's better to let him believe that I have something to lose in all this than for him to know that he's my best-kept secret.

Pilgrimage to the divine land

Drinking water from the cages of chained chests and fighting demons that aren't theirs to fight yet.

But I've also heard that love can sometimes be as familiar as laces from the same shoe that refuse to knot

like parallel lines racing towards each other but somehow never meeting

That's what soulmates are supposed to be.

And I guess that's okay because I've

Found comfort in knowing that opposites attract. and stand firm on the unbroken promises of God.

I've seen love die after 50 years together.

and I'm scared of giving myself to another to one day find me alone. And so, I'll maneuver the streets, picking at the objects of affection. For fear of tripping over my own feet. and blaming it on falling in love.

It's a beautiful thing that's not for me. And

I've been dodging Cupid for so long that I don't think he knows how to play hide and go seek.

Maybe one day all these silent harps will ring sweetly in my ear. Maybe one day an arrow with my name will draw somewhere near

Cupid may need help, but I'm never the best teammate, and my heart has never been in the open long enough to be caught. It's okay to be alone.

It doesn't mean I'm lonely; I'm just unsure of what is coming. If Cupid has an arrow, then I've got a double-barreled gun. And if he wants to play with hearts,

I've got 6 pairs of arms ready to escort this one so

May the best one win when it comes to the decision of forever after.

I can't feed off another woman's plate

I said I can't help her lick her wounds and rake my nails
through his spine as he paints my insides white
I can't feed off of another woman's plate
And one reality check of the world's values proves that I
can't be the wife subjected to Sharazades' tales either 'cause
Marriage doesn't have the sanctity it once held
See these females aren't scared of a married woman's
tears when he lines their pockets leaving her bones bare
by bedsides to use when these girls can't give him a place
to lay his worries I can't be the wife making closet space for
Torn veil mascara runs in pillowcases, lingerie that ain't
been touched by him but has so much red wine stains in
its corset, reminiscent of lonely days
Can't tell my children that the cold in this house won't stay
long when he ain't acknowledged my warmth in ages 'cause
he still treks four paws down hunting for anything he hasn't
damaged yet fetching everywhere but home, won't tell them
I can't keep the warmth in when he leaves entrances open
see
I refuse to be the hill he washes his body in when he brings
his fleas to the doorstep
But even then I prefer ownership than rentals, purchases
than credits so as much as I'd hate it
I still can't feed off another woman's plate
Can't anchor myself to that type of dharma
I possess a certain grace reputation pristine no man can
say I ever folded for him to lead me to destruction, but if
he leads right then I'll give him free reign

I can't feed off of another woman's plate can't shed my skin where she chokes out breathless gasps for more like she ain't accustomed to the air of pleasure or or or she believes this grip can seduce him into staying home longer than he knows to bust a nut

I can't feed off another woman's plate 'cause I know I'll come to regret the imprint she thrusted around his finger when I know the domino effect saw my momma live it daily punchline after punchline every time he mated with another still trying to wheeze out her breaths like he holds the secrets for her to breathe correct it seems like a world long gone before she became the other woman

I swear I can't feed off another woman's plate but the OG city girls claim to have the almanac were missing, they say when tag teamin' niggas the broke ones are always left behind teaching us to juggle the thirsty cause they're always willing and every so often the wifeys are left clueless to whatever woman shares her bed next

See we got the lessons but the blueprints are still lacking now mistresses feel they have some bad bitch glory like these men haven't proven to never leave and if you build your world in his you're more than likely going to bleed.

But no one ever stops to wonder what happens to his children in the midst of all this bloodshed. Leaving Tire marks on their happy homes, I can't feed off another woman's plate.

We don't share the same appetite and I'd be damned if I

have to floss the taste of her from my teeth 'cause I too get
to listen to a thousand and one tales sewer spat my way to
satiate my pain so it's impossible not to peep game when
you've watched the match regular
I won't chase a nigga either not entertaining the culture
of the bad bitch era I can't feed off another woman's plate
can't have his kids stepping on the same stools I step up to
can't raise my head when they admonish me in their gaze
Yeah mainly I worried 'bout giving a raise—sorry, getting
a raise—than raising them, see I just can't feed off another
woman's plate somehow our palates ain't aligned similar
like homophones yet so different they juxtapose

If I know nothing of love

I know it is never found in the arms of a man eager to seek
elevation
Yet I choose to settle despite the whispers in the cathedral
of safety built by the burning of your tongue, how can power
do anything but damage?

Dear Icarus, have we both flown too close to the sun or are
we both villains burning the letters of love for fear of the
fourth wall breaking?
If so, then let me rewind the narrative that is Joan of Arc
and become the Patron saint of my own heart
I wonder how Eliza reacted to the man who broke her heart

Was she as petty as Beethoven's composition for the lovely
Theresa Malfatti, a woman who rejected his proposal, did
he think making it harder for her to play would change her
mind?
Did Eliza choose to stay because of love or simply to prove
how strong she was for her son's sake?
I wonder if as she threw her trampled heart from the highest
skyscraper that was his crown, Was she truly blind or just
choose to keep her vision low
Just to protect herself from the misogyny that is history?

Words scrambling together just to make heartache more
common than need be
History is somehow riddled with unrequited love and men
clearing their name by killing the women they vowed to love

How distorted love truly is, yet I want nothing less than the darkness it is compounded of nothing less than short-lived peace as innocence fleets

I want the love that has us murderous
The love that makes me burn the world so you can't give it to someone else
I want the flames that dance across my skin at your touch so I am never cold
The type of fairy dust that makes infatuation a growing glow in my eyes
I want a love that would sacrifice the world just to save me the type of tragedies Shakespeare spoke of
The beauty of experiencing slow dives while everyone else drowns at our feet

I want the villain not the hero, for there is no limit or boundary that restricts the love of a villain when they give you their all
I want a love where even the darkest of moments seem like light in comparison

CHAPTER X
Domestic Affairs

"In situations of captivity the perpetrator becomes the most powerful person in the life of the victim, and the psychology of the victim is shaped by the actions and beliefs of the perpetrator."

~ Judith Lewis Herman, Trauma and Recovery: The Aftermath of Violence

Purple

I never learned to like The Color Purple, but I somehow got used to harmonizing for the symphonies of the raining on flesh from the love Harpo thought to teach Sophia, and I asked myself,
How does this love last longer than the currents of rivers?

How does my body Lecter itself into surviving anything close to attention?

Does it mean I am just another empty vessel strapping the definitions of the world on my shoulder and marching through camps with fists raised like white activists, not worthy of a Black woman's fight?

And should I learn to love myself before anyone else, I will start asking this body for permission.
I will start pampering it with survival before using it as a shield to mourn another.
I will stop yanking it from beds wrapped around four posters so it can stay planted on its knees.

Should I be a woman,
I will live with no life,
no pictures on the walls of my home,
no thoughtless souvenir or memorabilia as decoration to make me feel joy.

I will be woman whose main aim is to survive each day as

they come,
I will learn to love me enough to be a woman fueling
dumpster fires with amorphous arrows caught in vowels
propelling themselves by hangnails,
while the pile-driver of my lips subpoenas clusterfucks that
are sold to me as wonderlands by men who know nothing
of what women want...

or go through

Vows

My father found a home in the mess he made of his vows.
Birthed twelve to thirteen children
Most of which he never thought to own.
My father was once a hero-made villain. That's the thing
with fathers.
You never see them the way you ought to, and it leaves you
disappointed.
That Disney created fairytale images of something reality
doesn't even encourage.

My father sprinkled pain into my mother's tissues, made
her cry more than smile.
Said he loved her but never once thought of her as family.
I guess he needed someone to warm his bed while he gave
her a part of every woman, but never him.

My mother loved my father.
She placed seals and patches where her children might see
pain and silence, and she decorated it with love.
She had enough for them both. She never once talked
poorly. But she worked her hands to the core, as he worked
his hips to the whores.

I guess he thought if he sowed enough seeds between
weeds, she wouldn't be hostage to the thorns. I've heard
he laid his hands on her before she gave up on him.
Excuses overflow from her eyes as hatred burns in his.

My mother loved Brown,
and I guess it's because she's known dirt for a bit too long.
I've come to realize that Brown to her is for the anguished
nutrients of soils because
She was Gaia, and he was Atlas,
but he made the world around her fall.

My mother saw hidden figures in the darkness that weren't
there.
Fought with her shadow like Jacob and God, for she failed
to trust another woman's sweat in her pillows. Thought
that every whisper of the wind was a hushed moan in the
darkness.
Every plate he issued her heavy on the tongue, for women
have all eaten what she has. Have all been given portions
of him that only left her bitter and broken.

My father gave her what no other woman would take. Kept
introducing her to his sins, so she would pray him through
heaven's gates. He gave her tendons without muscles,
and force-fed her his appraisal.

But through it all, my mother never cried a tear. Raised her
voice plenty, but stood rooted in the same spot for far too
long. See, my mother was not a quitter, but she gave up
through struggling breaths while tying dirty laundry to thin
wires, should no one else see these women through them.

Eighteen years saw her grant him ultimatums,
but these women were brave.

My mother doesn't seem to care anymore. She fights
furniture in the shadows.
For those women have built their homes within her home,
left shredded skin in her way and on her couch. Have hidden
their souls in the cracks of her walls. Their
shallow breath beneath wooden furniture.

These women lived where she only visited,
tore her essence from the wall to claim their spot amongst
her children, and my mother cleaned up their mess for them.

All while never speaking ill of the man she loved. Yes
My mother bore it all.
But by now, she's had enough.

Why I left the dirty dishes in the sink

When they asked me why I left the dishes in the sink again, I stared at each facial feature and reminded them that it's easier to remember than it is to forget about the grease patterns painted into antique China that no one was supposed to use.

So, these dishes serve as a reminder of what I will no longer tolerate.

I told them that it's better to wait it out and wade in the water than it is to walk away from the bibliography you've written amongst the gasses of the galaxy.

I told them that we have all heard of love being so strong it could pull stitches, but no one told us that love is a miserable housemate
or that she could sometimes tear stents with magnetic fists and leave you crippled at the mercy of the ones you would die for.

I learned that when you're in love with someone who won't love you back, it's not so easy to run away from your shadow, and Mama reprimanded me for my answer.
She said she's been burned before, but she's also given up before, so she knows the disaster that occurs when rubber meets the road.
Mama said that I mistook the scars that resemble those from the implants of graft meets host as hard work,

and she's played it off as such so her kids don't see her sending the embers of her pride flying through war cannons.

She said the bootstraps of her self-worth were pulled by carriages filled with people who juggled life's fatal attraction like hot potatoes for circus tricks.
And my mama worked hard all her life but still couldn't see beyond the veil of prosperity.
That's why she taught me how to kiss something that broke you and heal something you never broke. My mama has the hands of an African healer and the love of a goddess flowing through her.

So I said, "Mama, I left the dishes in the sink because I figured I'd save myself the hassle of reenacting war and peace as the mortar to my home."

And Mama rearranged my life during her visit again.
She said, "Little girl, don't restart cycles; you don't have enough water to irrigate."
But she also showed me the immaculate designs I missed in my China, telling me why they were treasured.

I think you broke the China in me by replacing it with plastic replicas you forgot you stained.

I told her I'm still the same girl strapping herself to tether ball poles so she can mop the white horse from your lips.
I told her I restarted cycles to rinse the grease stains wrapped around my throat.

I told her that sometimes love isn't enough to live by.
I told her that I leave the dirty dishes in the sink because it
reminds me that something depends on my hard work. It
reminds me that sometimes love has to hurt, and the dirtier
I make it, the less value it eventually has. And that's a lesson
I'm going to force myself to accept, even if it means giving
myself a hernia.

Mama said I don't have to go through all she did.
Don't have to sing negro spirituals over each burial and
rebirth I ulcer myself into through the name of love and
support.
She said sometimes, most times the riders almost always
die before they are rewarded for their loyalty.
She said, I don't have to wrap you in a protective style for
fear you'd cheat on me, so in my ignorance, I hid the muse
you left behind on a Trojan horse where she wouldn't see
your boot prints on my back.

I couldn't show her that I had remission scars from the
discipline you gave me.
So I ate from the dirty dishes you served me,
and tried to find balance between weapon and weakness
when I stepped onto floors that had served as my bed for
ages.
I'm tired of feeling my heart refuse to beat when my chest
begins to weep.
So I said,
"Mama, I left the dirty dishes in the sink again because
someday I'll learn that they aren't worth the misery."

Flowers

I told him I didn't like flowers; it was a repetition of death that I couldn't live with.
A cancerous cell of hope hidden in poppies that auto-plays the memory of soldiers standing at attention in fields of gunfire.

I told him I don't like flowers because each time I see the withering of petals, I am forced to remember how the wreaths on caskets often fail in the morbid desires of perfuming bodies prepared as food for insects.

I told him that I don't like flowers because they force you to embalm the brokenness that no one speaks of when they place these displays on the homes that can't weather the storms.

I told him I don't like flowers because they clot the trigger of Raynaud in my vessels. I don't like flowers because a dying thing is not a way to show undying love.

but he adored art.
and I guess the irony of my hatred was poetic enough for him to sway me to his will.

And he bought me roses again today.

placed them on my weeping womb and said a Psalm of mourning for the things we conceived in the dark when

I thought this love was enough reason to swallow the placenta of women out of labor.

I never imagined seeing him place flowers on cells that were not here yet.

I told him I don't like flowers because they are a signal of impending doom. I don't like flowers because it is the only effort men make when they force you to overlook some unforgivable mistake. I don't like flowers because they make you second-guess moving on.

He said he brought flowers so that he could grieve our loss before he truly lost his temper and lost me.

And in my hunger for love, I accepted that it was the thought that counted, not how much I hated this motif of destruction. I think that sometimes love is supposed to hurt. but I don't know when I came to that conclusion.

I don't know when I stopped being me and became someone he wanted to be with, but I know it was the fear of being alone.

He said, "Baby, these roses are an apology for using your blood as natural paint for my pieces."

He said my tears were the primary gloss that brought his portraits to life, and my breath hanging from his fingertips was immortal enough to make him feel like I was nothing without him.

He said I should know that he does this out of love because each step he has taken since I got here is a stagnant consequence of knowing me, and he touched the shades of blue streaked across my face with the very tips of the brush he used.

Did I tell you he loved art?
So much so that he illustrated the personification of chaos and raging storms in the citadel of my heart?

I have learned to love flowers because every day he gives me one, and by the time they start to droop, I am caught nursing each scorpion and leech he inserted into me as punishment for the sun shining back towards my children's unmarked graves, which this world wouldn't see.

I guess he took Tanya Tucker seriously and brought my flowers into my days,
hoping to show me how fragile life was because the withering of flowers was a markdown he placed on my life. He told me where he'd store my bones should he stare tomorrow into her eyes and never find me there.

So I went to the altar, where he consummated the marriage of flesh and soil with flowers I had never learned to appreciate,
I told him I don't like flowers.
But I guess I didn't speak loud enough for him to comprehend the meaning of my tears and my fears.

So hear me now:
I don't like flowers because the dead cannot reside with the living.

Limited

She said she knows when she has reached her limit, but she's nowhere near it because she still treads carefully on the tripwires of his anger to avoid the fists.

She said she learned to be attentive so she knows when he's changing before her eyes, and if he does, then she has no problem showing him the door.

She can handle herself, but she'd rather not.
She's been through enough bullsh*t to know how to dish it back. She told herself that she's not trapped; she's only staying this long because you taught her the meaning of pleasure when you first laid her back and placed her needs before yours, fixed her leaky kitchen faucet, and forced her to choke on the collared greens from your garbage disposal, she doesn't realize that was when you first met her.

When you were the prince and not the villain, she cant see the difference now, so she said she loved it when you sent vibrations of recycled mellow yellow tunes into her tied tubes, and she's into kinks that have her playing submissive as long as you are the dominant factor, and apparently that gives you the right to beat her, neglect, and mistreat her.

She said there are more than nine clouds, and she wants to take you on a journey to the furthest one. See, baby girl doesn't know that she can live life without a man,

So she nods submissively when he says that he better be the only one kissing her scars away, and he kisses them in such detail as if she doesn't know herself, as if she can't love herself, as if she won't treat herself the same way he does. as if these scars weren't his doing to begin with

He's the communion she can't get enough of, and that's a shame. He painted her lips black and blue to match the raccoon-like tones around her eyes, and her thighs got scratches that didn't come from true love.
He gaslights and manipulates, and when he's done, she's left singing sorry to the wind, adopting all his faults and raising them as her own. She's so in love with him that she doesn't see the sky crying for her sake.

Baby girl doesn't want to be lonely, so she puts up with the torture, and if her breath is labored, then she has enough air to stick around for the encore because she's never fully conscious when he's done with his lectures consistently hitting pulse points trying to beat his point across and he swears he's a man.

Thing is, he's always going to be less than.

I said recalcitrant

I never knew how much love could be compounded into
such small frames
How its forcefield could dunk me beneath all realms of pain
I never knew how much I needed this suffering, this sweet
balm resembling a fiery worship to consume me
Until I walked with my heart on a platter serving it
to your people
Make believing it was my dreams of the future left there
in the open
So slander my name on its creases 'cause I no longer take
all your punches, but I can't forget all the things we've been
through so as it happens
I'm still lost in time, and you asked if I'm selfish enough to
leave all this history behind
I said I used to put my heart on the line for you
Used to watch her burn as I shelter your pain, now I got no
more love to give
See, this ash ain't worthy of rebirth but I'm building a future
where I can see the sunshine for once
I'm building a wealth through which I can tell my
grandchildren I survived
I survived the worst heartache had to offer and I'm still here
standing strong so I'll make believe I'm strong, 'cause one
day I'll be the lesson you never forget
One day I'll be the one whose breath is a threat
boy, I don't forgive unless I can forget and I'm just not that
strong of a woman yet, I'm just not that strong of a woman
yet

Her backbone

She thought that somewhere there was a warrior she would find if she was pushed to get her hands dirty and extract her spleen as a weapon to defeat the infection holding the reins of her life.

It turns out that it depends on where you draw the line and the horizons you're able to see, And a couple years ago, she couldn't see over the adrenaline while in the speed chase of Madea and OJ because she claimed to only ride with the best

Yes, she met a couple veterans that taught her how to savor the smell of gunpowder and sizzling flesh should the father figures she threw flags at be disappointed that she gave so much at her peak.

you see

Her mother kept her hands clasped and her eyes so far away, looking around heaven, that she never saw what Eli missed in his own home. She was 10 when she heard that virgin's blood cures AIDS.

And she remembered Cyntonia Brown and thought that self-defense was no defense, so she took a knee to the neck like a champ, telling herself that there were only two ways this could have gone:

He didn't mean it because he didn't see her through his mommy issues, and her daddy issues kept her begging for his approval.

What a fucked-up way to live!

When he gave her what he couldn't lose, she vowed that she'd repay the favor while professing love on latex seats to the landlord of her body. And he built his business on principle, collecting payment on delivery every night while she cries in corners that one day these nights won't see her mimicking missionaries and eagles.

She's twelve, and he still leads her to bedsides like a father handing over a daughter at an altar,
Watching her tease every saint and sinner rough enough to punch the timecards in her young eyes until the black merges into purple shades of ecstasy.

She cried in the confessional at fourteen and said that she built her house on sand.
And when she finally got away from his grasp, she saw the red eyes of customers she didn't know were preachers busting hell's doors wide open yet exiling people like her from their safety behind pulpits as if there was a pull-out method when sinning.

She said she's nobody's black sheep.
She didn't do this on her own accord; a child stolen from her sheets and forced to learn the trades of the streets cannot be so undeserving of God.

but

no one wants to hear that.

Now she's sixteen, a lady of the night but a mother at her day job.

She's that Cinderella from the ghetto, sporting purple hair, a bruised knee, and red talons used for striking across men's cheeks. She says it's her art because she was
the canvas for his
And
She's got to somehow have identification to give to these kids. She has to use the lessons to survive.

She's 18 and she's working less than minimum wage.
She never finished elementary , but she has ambitions because she does this for them so that they won't learn a beggar's grip.
She said she taught her girls to pray, but never on their knees. Telling them that they'd always be the butt of a joke because they can't wield limp prosthetic dicks
And
She keeps her head high like she's a queen, even when she feels filthy inside, because
No excuse she makes can help her this time.

She's got promises to fulfill because everybody knows that DNA only proves that Daddy is not available,
because it's Mama's baby, and street walkers have enough respect for themselves to go looking for somebody whose wallet was only good for one night of picking

So she spits twice for payment and laps it up to feed the child she has to keep.

Yes,

She's got a backbone dug from the hands of the boys in blue because she's got to do what every mom has got to do. And I heard that

She found her backbone lining the streets to the past like lost trails to her one phone call home if she ever finds herself in a bind. She counts the change and feeds her child. While she strangles the thought,

Telling herself she'd rather sell all her organs to feed stray dogs than go back to people who never believed and let them see the hurt they caused.

She's doing better for hers because no one did right by her. and her girls won't know these damaged street signs by name.

And until she draws her last, they won't have to suffer at the hands of men or women, no matter who they claim to be.

When I cut the dead end of my hair

I snipped away the wounds[31], springing new leaves on my chest,
and thought that I could replace the identity the cold stole from me.
I tore my paranoia from my tongue and scolded her for hiding behind realism for years, so that I couldn't identify her pessimism,
because if you camouflage yourself into a set fantasy long enough
You become it, or it becomes you.

I watched my beauty take turns somersaulting through mirrors, trying to find the fairness when her hair wasn't there to compliment the harshness of her cheekbones.
Watched my melanin scream "nappy head" and "bald head" and bought scarves to hide the decision I stood by.

When I cut my hair to hide behind scarves, the fountain of my pen found the meaning of Judges 16:22, and drought settled over the cries of hunger for words that my clogged veins couldn't identify as famine but as thawed resourcefulness.

When I cut my hair to lose sight of my fading identity, I ripped my body in two halves, pushed one under my mattress, and took one as the new me.
Now I search the one hidden for reference to the road I took to be here and say to hell with beauty or identity because I have freedom, and that's all I could have asked for the day

31 *"The past beats inside me like a second heart." ~ John Banville*

I finally cut my hair.

CHAPTER XI
Faith

"The Bible is the greatest of all books; to study it is the
noblest of all pursuits; to understand it,
the highest of all goals."

~ Charles C. Ryrie

When I go to church

I wonder if the woman catapulting tongues of praise from the raw sludges of her mouth knows that the reason God is silent is because she has become so accustomed to speaking over him,
Has become so focused on seeking attention and glory that she never stops long enough to listen
Has ran past the mile marker where she should have patiently awaited the comforter
and she says that her baritones cause earthquakes in oceans because he is more deaf and ancient than savior,
and mercy, more vengeful than the saints he want us to emulate,
and sometimes he becomes fugitive she is bound to claim, becomes missing in action and she cannot rely on him

and she speaks over everyone with a difference of opinion

I said I wonder if he ever thought to write her letters, or speak a tone louder than hers
and she says sometimes, her faith becomes invalid
sometimes she believes this is only a ploy made for the mad to believe in something other than themselves
and she holds onto that because she desperately needs something to believe in

When I go to church,
I watch women become Huldah,
and Miriam's jealousy is evident before conferment,

and I watch the split curtains become redundant covenant
in her eyes as the altar becomes gap for her own powers
to save and bring everyone's attention to her magnitude
instead of God

instead of salvation

instead of mercy or holiness

When her tongues split in church she becomes slithering
validation for saints and sinners
And heaven and hell
She becomes the interpreter of God's 400 years of selective
mutism

She becomes the understanding of why he is suddenly silent

It's so hard to pray sometimes

[32]'Cause when I'm down here on my knees I catch myself resurrecting these scars billowing worries in this haze of a mind
and my voice is so sore from screaming "mercy please," begging God not to break me this time.

So,

If a prayer is just a word then saying "heal this mind before you touch my heart" is no short request
or "twist this heartbreak laboring through me into the deafness of Decapolis, let me be mute to the principalities bound on destroying more than just flesh" wondering if he would look kindly on such colored request or remind me of Luke 18:10-14

So I'm silently down here on my knees like Daniel wondering, what do I say to the father if I should pray these sins backsliding into promiscuity?
Tell me, should I go pressing them into his nail prints or recite the Lord's Prayer and forget the ABCs beaten into me in Sunday School?

So I say "God, it's so hard to stay focused when I'm halfway through with
this blessing and still pivoting on the precipice of damnation." I don't know how the righteous do this but I feel forsaken, feel sometimes like I will never make it though I consistently

seek to dream it.

It's easier than actually pushing forward

See, when I work towards it I keep falling flat, now I'm left hoping that like John he'll somehow meet me where I'm at.

I'm still trying though
Still trying to be the change they need to see to know you're real
Can't forget to remember the days I spent afraid of being on my knees
I'm not reborn yet
I'm still facing the repercussions of one man's disobedience contributing to my baptism into death

God I'm nothing like JOB, so if this is a test then I'm a brethren in Athens using the seeds on the wayside
Believing without seeing that's faith, and I want to think that I'm full of it but yet still I find myself staring at the inscription to the unknown God knowing without a doubt that eyes have not seen anything short of your glory.

I have an ear so I have heard what the spirit says in the scriptures, yet I'm struggling against this chokehold of fear paralyzing me into complacency and somehow I know this red cord doesn't save me unless I face prosecution instead of hiding from the noose hell bound in keeping me in darkness.

Its so hard to pray sometimes

for I have yet to keep watch for a bridegroom knowing I have to first unlock this cryptogram of understanding before I can ascend into it's true meaning

It's so hard to pray sometimes
when I'm waking up in fear of being bound by my own belt and delivered to the foes of the land, see I don't know if I'm ready to be imprisoned or face death for what I know to be right despite the promises assuring me of a greater inheritance that I lack the sight to see, I'm walking blind in this land

And I'm running out of oil for this lamp, don't have enough to spare
So if I have vandalized a hiding space for it's words on my heart then why do I still think mythology's cute when it's oracles are nothing compared to the Delphi of the Bible?

32 *"If you know the enemy and know yourself, you need not fear the result of a hundred battles. If you know yourself but not the enemy, for every victory gained you will also suffer a defeat. If you know neither the enemy nor yourself, you will succumb in every battle." ~ Sun Tzu, The Art of War.*

Prayer allows you to know the enemy, to know who God is and to have discernment of the spirit and understanding. Hence, prayer may never be easy or pretty or fluid because worship and walking with God will forever be an unending battle.

Purple

See, I'm no goddess but I have dreamt of living in the
shadows of the mighty
have posed for statues and envisioned purple robes
of royalty

and he told me I was celestial told me that my body was
coated in ceramic and marble
told me I was good enough to eat from the hands of God
that the latrine in my mouth was proof enough that the
beast that lived within me could be tamed

gave me a new name and forged words from volcanic seas
that promised lies
and I guess I should have known that
I became a target the minute I spoke to him

my part-time Romeo zipped up the mess he made of me
and told me that fearing death would teach me that shallow
graves and bore holes were one and the same, that lava
burnt in veins and acid could quench the thirst of the broken
hearted

See, revenge isn't a dish I've grown to like, but I've never
seemed to like the fact that I rejected him, that they hunted
owls and left me searching for wisdom in the bedsheets
of Solomon, but he said I was royal and that my royalty
surpassed those of kings before me.

I should have known that purple letters weren't poison, but the boundaries of royalty and loyalty were spun together by the tests of perception.

I should have known that sins are greater than asteroids headed towards earth. The beauty in our struggles is that in the age that this all falters, your letters will remain etching themselves in the spaces secluded for the people of God, reminding me that I am noble, that he is royalty, and that my hands have borrowed the moral compass of angels so that God could breathe salvation into my sickle-shaped essence, thus evading earth's destruction.

Yes, the letters of Paul, you may know, but let me introduce you to the woman with 66 purple letters of love.

Woman anonymous

Someone once asked me who I was.
Said woman, you lay beneath stars as if waiting for the
moonlight to heal you.
Your hands are blood-stained like Jael's
And you walk around with your womb shackled to the
reaper.

Has God not heard you yet?

Lord, they called me mad for waiting for me to wrestle with
you. But I was waiting to touch the hem of your garment.
And they ask me, Why wait on someone who may never
come?

So, I told them to call me Mary, for I have broken men who
have roamed the streets of my thighs just to leave with
venom in their mouths.

So I believe that in eluding salvation and ruining empires
I have formed bridges to the fireplaces of Sodom and
Gomorrah.

I am woman scorned, waiting to be seen.
Woman calling out to God, hoping that in each coffin I lay,
he will find the seals of destruction. Enough to come and
save me.
Enough to hear my pleas

I am woman at the well, drawing water from dried-up brooks once filled with the bitter tears of Rachel.

I am Rahab, pillaging through the ruins of my Babylon.
Spying a tornado of feelings beneath my chest
I am woman not worthy of love, but somehow laid spread across the altar, for he has heard me.

Has taken all seven deadly sins
has seen me sacrifice myself to be whole again.

I am woman once laughed at by Elkanah.
Woman fearless with the weight of a nation on her shoulders.

I am woman, anonymous, but still on his radar.

Woman anointing the feet of God

I am woman, whole and forgiven.
I am woman eating bread and drinking from the flask of amnesty.
My comforter is here.
My waiting has ended.

See, I am Sarai, holding onto the bundled promises of God that I once laughed at.
I am Naomi, leading Ruth home once again.
I am Haggar trodding through the wild.

For
I am woman building temples within my kingdom
an 'A' inscribed for atonement.

I am woman whole and worthy.

The cemetery between my thighs has lost its pull.

So I told them that I was woman bruising the head of the
serpent.

I am woman holding onto the hands of God and winning.

Who God is to me?

I tried learning your name again to show them how much
you mean to me.
Tried reshaping your essence so I could trap you in a bottle
and keep you on display, but it didn't work.

It turns out you like to roam the streets,
like to be in prisons, bars, and whorehouses, and I don't do
that scene, but each name you have comes only for those
who frequent the dilapidated reserves of this earth you've
created.

I guess you really only came for the sick and broken, not
just in the parables, and we can't act as if we saw Jehovah
Rapha without being raw and truthful,
but I keep pretending that's not how you met me,
acting like we met in a church and my gowns were always
washed in the blood.

I tried to follow your request, but I keep hitting dead ends.
I'm not sure if I'm introducing you to the right crowd or if it's
because they can't see you when I fail to give a testimony of
Jehovah Tsidkeenu, so I began to do some cleansing.

I changed my lesson plan but not my dressing to show that
Jehovah Qadash was my blessing, and I hope this method
works.

And if they ask me your name this time, I'll know to Introduce

them to Genesis, where we first met, and make them use
it as an icebreaker.

I'll tell them I believe because you've proven Genesis 17 for
in my days of torment you are my El Shaddai, and if I ever
get dumbfounded when they ask for a single name, then I'll
tell them that you are God and cannot be described by the
words of man, but should they learn your name, they'd have
to read your journal to know for themselves
that you are never changing and always worth it.

See, you Jehovah Shammah is helping me to forget past
sorrows and mistakes, to forgive seventy times seven, so I
don't rush through my days. I'll let tomorrow take care of
herself so I can be as free as Lillies in the field.

And if they don't understand why I loved you, then Genesis
2 tells no lies;
you are my Jehovah Elohim, my creator on high, you breathe
the breath of life into me from dust,
so I have highlighted Genesis 15 for them, where I prove just
how much you are still Adonia Jehovah, Psalm 95 Jehovah
Asah, no time can change your words, and isn't that just
exceptional?
Because Isaiah 45 solidifies that you are Jehovah. Yeah, you
are the rock I'll tell stories about.

Lord, I don't think I learned all this from men speaking in
the confounded tongues of Babel.
I think I first knew of Jehovah Jireh when I saw you providing
more than the ram in Genesis 22, making all my wildest

dreams come true. I never went hungry when all my needs were filled by you.

It seems to me you've been working for centuries, and I'm not the only one you've assisted, so like Exodus 17, I call you Jehovah Nissi, hoping one day your banner will be in the seven churches on the four corners of the world, where I can wave it and not only let my light shine for those close by to see it.

I hope you don't mind that I told them you were always my Jehovah Shalom, when I fought depression and my mental health,
And I know that when I lay crippled by fear and sickness, you were keeping me sober and grounded should I give into the pressure. So I tell them to call you Jehovah Eylon, call you Jehovah Tsaba, for you are my Jehovah Rohi searching for me each time I stray.

I tell them I am still that missing sheep, and you, my Shepard have not stopped searching since I strayed some 10 years ago.

I am worth it and though your timing may not be mine you are my Jehovah Eloheenu, the same Jehovah spoken of in Exodus 20
You are the same God that led Abram from Ur,
Noah in the ark,
Jesus on the cross and John to the new Jerusalem
You are God everlasting and you are the MC of my faith.

But if, when I am done, they still have no idea who you are, then I will simply tell them that you are who you are to me. Almighty God, you are still a sovereign master, an eternal creator
A holy one
My provider, My banner, My peace, My healer,
My righteousness, My sanctifier,
The lord of host Ever present
Lord most high
My shepherd
My maker
My God

My God, you are all you are and more and I am proud to know you by your name.

The greatest man I ever knew

The bravest man I've ever known said he loved me and somehow meant it.

The bravest man I've never met held my hands in his each day, urging me to carry on. He taught me that he could fix my broken bones and use them to make me a home. Took my calloused hands and blew breath into me so that I may one day remember to thank him long enough that I can somehow imagine his voice whispering John 3:16 in the hollow roots of my chest.

He taught me love, though I could never stop long enough to love him or know him.

He gave me so much more than I ever offered him.

The bravest man I'll one day meet wore more purple medallions than any mortal man who tried to win my heart, and I heard that drum beating like the deafening gallop of horses as he hid my heart where only he could touch it.

I saw him twist ropes together, pulling my limp body from the wells of depression. And I felt his pain as he watched me lay beneath naked stars that wept for my plight. I heard him say his yolk was easy. And I cried to the only man who would ever heal me.

He taught me how much I could give him, and he would still love me.

Taught me that he was mine and that his armor was bloodstained for me. And I knew I'd found my knight. He

bled for me, so I wouldn't have to bleed alone.
And somewhere along the lines, I took him into tombs so
I could hide him from the world. because I didn't want to
share with him, but he didn't want to stay there.

He was the greatest man I've ever known.

The only man I'll ever love
And I made him miss me while I stood in his presence
each day.
I remember all he's done, but I can't remember once
making him proud.
I spent so long scratching at his face so I could escape
his embrace.
And as my trembling hands made for his throat, I didn't
stop to reflect that in killing the man I couldn't touch, I
was killing something within me that meant way
too much.
I've lived and not loved, but he died for those he loved.
And I want to say I'm sorry to the man I was too afraid of
highlighting.
I wish I could hear the cheering of angels, as they watch
this earth adore you.

What I'd give to hear you say you love me once more.
What I'd give to swallow your word.

I'm sorry for leaving. I promise this time I'll stay.
But a heart that's been broken need not hide
from your gaze.

Pink Roses

I promised myself that if I was ever going to fall in love, I'd get myself a happy ending.

And because I never had a role model bringing roses to the women in their presence, I imagined that somehow my Prince Charming was stuck at a red light and couldn't pass until I looked Cupid in the eyes and gave him permission to alter my heart.

I never thought I was good enough for pink roses. So, I told myself to stop and feel the breeze. Live in the moment, because even Shakespeare knew that somehow love was never worth it.

And then I met you.

You who spoke softly but with authority, created love out of nothingness and took control of my life as you told me how much you loved me. You were the one I was afraid to break my walls for, so you climbed over and stayed lonely with me. You said you died for me when no one else would. Said you'd hold my hand and fight Piranhas for me. But I considered myself a waif.

Rejected you time and again, and yet you still came to my rescue the minute I fell to my knees, telling me that no woman as beautiful should ever be that low.

Now I don't need roses, for I've got the greatest gift of all: comfort, warmth, and love from afar.

Traffic lights didn't stop him
The color red made him charge at me with force because
I was his goal. I guess dreams do come true.

For the man I speak of, he never once asked for anything
but my soul. And yet he told me that he loved you too.
He was not only for me, but he gave me every attention I'd
need.

This polyamorous relationship made me jealous of everyone
else he paid attention to.
He said you left him for someone else but told me to tell
you that when you're ready, you should call him.
And he'll be right there waiting for you.

I've had a picture saved for years

The only words on a paper full of tears: Dear Jesus

So dear Mr. Jesus,
I've been here so many times that I literally have book pages
smudged with fear.

Dear Mr. Jesus,
I never thought to write to you.
Can you pull the drawbridge of wonder and innocence and
tell me the best sanction for these developments?

Dear Mr. Jesus,
I'm still doodling your name in a boatful of tears with no
oars.
Tell me If the ceiling breaks, will the house collapse on me,
or will you show me my figure outside it standing before
the new doors of temporary homes?

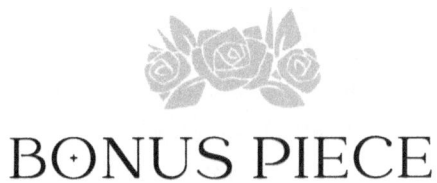

BONUS PIECE

The story is told of a serial killer who used rib cages as windchimes[33]

and it made me privy to the knowledge that all criminals, when just starting out, keep souvenirs to remember the mess of their formative years, and I realized that if I kept reminiscing on the past, then I was just another walking trophy of how he laid siege to the mind and damaged the future.

But if I were optimistic, I would see that everything terrible gives way to a terrifyingly beautiful outcome, for those chimes gave music no one else would.

But I'm not optimistic,
So I thought that if I kept showing how affected I was, then I was just another win for the man who took my childhood.

So, I will not be affected instead
this is a eulogy to the woman in me who sat at window

seats for six years to farm the bones of everything that girl became before she gained strength to dig the spleen of healing uprooted from the tenor of harmonies excluded from society, and she peels back thick layers of epidermis to expose years of planning that show the undertones of my auto-tuned reality to harpies whose drumbeat dismantles sensibility.

She realizes that by enabling her anger, she becomes that girl she never wished to be, and so she does laundry cycles to wash that jinx from her life.

So shout out to this woman, whose musty corners range from the extremities of turbo pumps to piercing guns; this woman, whose back is told never to trust its own spine and support system;

this woman, whose mind designed the encryptions of the dark web;
this woman, who watches the day go by without even considering anything outside the
dome.

Shout out to the woman who saw dawns and never sunsets, the one who prayed for the nights to end as hands groped her undeveloped chest, and he said he knows she is awake even when her subconscious drums up the buzz of anything else to take focus off of what is happening.

This woman who decapitates the girl who is aggressively

questioned like a culprit by the justice department and never once thought to remind them that this mess never came from her hands every time her memory rises with the Saharan dust—shout out to that girl shifting identities as if it were the norm.

The girl who laughed at every joke like it was ok and smiled at everything past the normal range

That girl who was a no talent dimwit maligned by the egomaniacs of the world

That girl wired to distrust that anyone could find love in her

Shout out to that girl who spoke of her home life like she lived in paradise just so no one would question her about the secrets of life that hang in the balance.

This is the woman years took to sharpen
The woman whose combinations are not flooded by the digital analytics absorbed from her past
That girl who took social sciences, religion, and myths to encourage this woman

So shout out to this woman who has a cyclone of scorpions giving her shelter.

This woman exercised her right to speech by removing tissue paper from her lips and stripping it of its elasticity, and shout out to

That girl who never became the girl she feared but died long ago so this woman could stand reborn from those bones planted where no one may find them

A phoenix still unable to find herself, but she is not yet giving up on this woman who stays paranoid, but she is getting there
And this woman will make damn sure that she is never that girl again or becomes that girl.

This woman will take the world by storm even if she has to keep farming her bones, tears, and blood by the wayside, I promise you that.

33 "Speak to me of things the world has yet to truly understand, of the instant meaning of each bird's call, of a child's secret thoughts in her mother's womb, of the measured rhythmical time of every man and woman's breath, of the true colors of the inside of the moon, of the larger miracles in small things, the deeper mysteries."

~ Edwidge Danticat, The Farming of Bones

I NEVER STOP WRITING

until the pain in my chest becomes a heart attack.

until I see them frown and rub defibrillators to bring me back from the edge of a great story;

until the minus before my name becomes the promise of a positive p affirming the possibility of my grandmother's blessings on me

until my fingers are no longer visible virile flesh yearning to pluck Shakespeare's most glorified tragedy from Anthony's chest; until writing becomes my Brutus forever jailing me between justice and betrayal

until I stand before my dreams and say to the world that I made it with all of me intact, without giving my past shelter in my future

I never stop writing until the skies become a blinding blue, baking the hope of clear days with a sprinkle of love in the optimism of rainbows that go the distance to make me proud of myself.

make me want to re-walk all the lines that were trials turned triumphs. that were plastic shrapnel to destinations of luck that were great achievements worth mentioning in newsletters

And I believe that If I never stop writing, then I can see how the other half lives.

How every roadblock becomes a stepping stone; how every mirror talk becomes doses of strength of courage of hope; how this all becomes a reality that I can own bragging rights to

How this all becomes another way to stick it to the world and say checkmate bitch, I win

ACKNOWLEDGMENTS

Firstly, I must acknowledge the almighty God and his never-ending grace and mercy, which are driving forces in my life.

To the first two people who made me realize I loved literature and writing by putting me at the forefront of public speaking. All our speech practices for JCDC paid off in my life. I will forever market my love of poetry to you because you remind me of all the ways I could write and perform to bring life to words. You will forever be the secret ingredient in my writing and my performances. So, here is to you, Reverend Gordon Cowans and Mrs. Constance Malcolm. I have learned innumerable things from you both.

Your name may not be on the dedication, but it is because of you and your need to understand that I had the heart to disclose certain personal pieces. This would have been impossible without your impact. You are so much more than an acknowledgement, and we may not be close, but you are the reason this is completed and published. You sat through many doubts, tears, confusion, anger, mental breaks, and ailments, and you celebrated it all when I failed to find the energy to. You have always been my only light since we were younger, and even now you shine enough for me to do the same. We may never see eye to eye, but know that I will always respect you, no matter how many times I say I hate you. Love you immensely K.O.H.

To Reverend Earl Thames and his impact on my ever growing love for writing and the need to seek out and explore varying worlds and characters through books.

To Orane Hanson for all those nights you stayed behind to accompany me home after extra class. To our memories made inside and outside of MHS. The majority of my extra CSEC subjects would have been impossible without your support.

To O'Shane Smikle, thank you for everything over the years, but most of all, for my nieces and nephew.

To my only nephew, my one starboy, my muse and little helper. The love I have for you is beyond any other. You are intelligent, fierce, protective, loyal, and oh so much trouble, but you are one of the best children—despite how many times you are scolded. You will forever be cherished, loved, and appreciated for your radiance exudes all else. I love you A'mir.

To A'Zaria, in everything you do, never dim the light in you. I pray that you will find a world filled with laughter, joy, and memories that ignite an unquenchable fire for the never-ending holiday in your head. May your admirable imagination never run out of fuel, and your well of creativity never run dry.

To my greatest blessing, my unwavering inspiration, my newest source of happiness, my niece Tiny. You have taught me a lot in these months, and I anticipate your growth and all the challenges and frustrations you will one day offer. I can hardly wait on you to be one and talk and walk.

To all my siblings and their significant others: thank you.

To my first niece Jayla Hall, I love you

To my little brother from another family, Danté Elliot, it was a pleasure watching you grow over the years and having memories I still laugh at today. I hope you are forever doing well, CJ.

To my relatives—all my aunts, uncles, and elderly cousins, given to me, chosen by me, accepted by me, reimagined with me—who never gave up on me when I gave up on myself, I appreciate you.

To a few of the many women who had a hand in raising the person I am: Aunty Doreen (RIP), Aunty Juliet (RIP), Aunty Pam (RIP), Ner, Donna, Vel, Aunty Jasmine (and her sister Anette), Aunty Stacey, and Aunty Pet, thank you for whatever lessons I took from you, no matter the length of my guardianship.

To: Ashley Ricketts, Morgan Foster, Colleen 'Abby' Ricketts, Rhea-Divine Perry, Tavielle Williams, Racquea Melville, Leandra Hall, Sukya Williams, Tony Mitchelle, Tianna Antonio, Charles-Marie Young, Aaliyah Simpson, Taina McKenzie, Nadjah-Lee Williams, Rickay Davis, Regina Gayle, Janel Cunningham, Ashalee Brown, Amanda Williams, Sejavia Campbell, Omelia Daley, Breannah Edwards, Sydoni Maitland, Rianna Walters, Shanique Fletcher, Sejavia Campbell, Jullianna Powell, Shaznae Howe, Donae Solomon, Trayon Martin, Carlton Barrett, Tarique Treasure, Andre Rowe, Renardo Raynor, Kimani Williams, Andre Greene, Samuel Morally, Nkosana Denton, Alex Patmore, Miguel Williams, Roshawna Bartley, Zachery Bryan, Monique Rowe-Carter, Courtney Carty, Brenique White, Francine Miller and so, so many more. We may be miles apart and have undoubtedly grown apart from each other. We may no longer talk, but thank you for some of the most memorable times I treasure today.

To the friends who looked out for me and accompanied me to every off-campus after-school class: Gary Lloyd Foster, Machael Blair, Orain Solomon, Carey Blair, and Dane Flemming, thank you.

To Jaynelle Burchell, Denvor Green, Jewel Virtue, and Krissann Gayle, thank you for loving the craft so much that you became an inspiration and avid reader and audience member on many blocked nights and through many doubtful and frustrated moments.

To the ones who always looked out for me, notwithstanding my stubborn ways: Miss Nissan Gentles, Mr. Ricardo Smith, Mrs. Sharon Wilmot-Simpson, and Mr. Leroy Fearon, thank you for educating and mentoring me as a parent and confidant away from home. I respect and appreciate you always and forever, and one day I'll make you proud to have had me as a student.

The ones who believed I could do whatever I put my mind to, the ones who believed I was talented beyond measure: Kenrick Hanson, Bianca Dempster, Danielle Francis, Alyssa Mcleish, Takiyah Edwards, Ramon Stultz, Orane Hanson, Abigail Thompson, and Karalia Carr, thank you for giving me the strength to believe in myself and for loving and embracing the things I do and love. It has inspired me countless times; without you, this would not be possible.

To Uncle Richard, Uncle Mickey, Aunty Bev, Sis. Evadney Dempster, Aunty Gean, Aunty Queenie, Aunty Pat, Sis. Karen, and Aunty Dion.

To the 2007-2013 cohort of Knox Junior School (who I started with).

To the 2013-2014 cohort of Knox Junior School (who I graduated with).

To the original members of Manchester High School's Form 1-4 class of 2014 and Form 2-4 class of 2015.

To Miss Gentle's Unit 2 Literatures in English class 2019, and the plethora of people I interacted with during my year at Knox College (Thonesia Jarrett, Jessica Stone, Courtney Carty,Ryan Mullings, Jodeen Blake, Tallia Clarke, Saffia White, Zoey Haynes,Donisha Wright, Teneshia White, Kamoy Allen, Shanoy Thompson, Ashaura Campbel, Shawn Dale, Jordan Mccnowell, Ronald Robinson, and many more).

To Shericka Rose, her sister Novia, the twins Sasha and Sara and Shemay McDonald amongst many others who contributed to memories at Friday night youth services at Spaulding Gospel Assembly from 2013 to 2017.

To the original Manchester High School scholars class, our mentors and our mentees, thank you.

To all the Sunday School class members of Beulah Missionary Church of Ritchies Jamaica I grew up with 1994-2020 (Shaedee Dempster, Richard Brown, Destiny Marshall,, Kellian Morris, Toriann Elliot): thank you all for the infinite memories.

To Paris and Shay/Shaquan.

To all my Sunday School teachers at Beulah Missionary Church over the years (Aunty Pat, Sis. Karen, Chrissy, Sis. Amy, Mrs. Bonner, and Pastor Dalkeith Bennett).

To all the VBS and youth fellowship teachers at Spaulding Gospel Assembly and Light of the World Worship Center who taught me more than their fair share of lessons. (Nurse Smikle,Sis Dhalia,Sis Marcia)

To Rheanna Perrin, we have never been that close, but thank you for consistently sending those messages that were always right on time. I appreciate them more than you will ever know.

To Miguel Williams (Miggy Wiggy) thank you for the times you encouraged me.

To Shawna-Gaye Bailey, Chardonnay Francis, Saskia Williams, and Timothy Gilbert: thank you.

To Nastassia Mason-Wilson and Marvia Scott-Tulloch, thank you.

To all the teachers who ever taught me (Knox Junior 2007-2014, Manchester High 2014-2019 & 2021, and Knox College High 2019-2020), thank you to those who are no longer in my life but aided me in becoming the woman I am by taking too many chances on me when I didn't.

To my neighbors who aided in some way or another Mr. and Mrs. Reid, Mr. Green (RIP) and Mrs. Green, Mr. and Mrs. Blair, Mr. and Mrs. Thomas, Mrs. Walker, Donna, Granville, Jeffrey, Kartel, Steve Ms. Graham (Aunt sis RIP), and Brother Grant and his wife Aunty Sher.

And to those I unintentionally forgot to mention along the way because I cannot possibly name every individual, I appreciate you and am incredibly sorry. Love you.

And to you, thank you for supporting me through this purchase and reading. I hope you found it fulfilling.

AUTHOR'S NOTES

My pieces are mostly written in the first person; only two handfuls are personal piecesthe majority are character made. The majority of the poems in this collection were culled from an old poetry notebook in which I had been composing since I was fourteen. This is a change because those components are no longer found in the writing of a more mature craft. A force is only as powerful as you allow it to be, and writing has proven to be just that..

'*For my friend's mother,*' I had no name for this piece and still don't. I tried calling it the *Martyrdom of a Mother,* but I didn't. It is a poem I never shared with anyone, until recently, and I'm still not certain how I will feel about publishing it. Written for my friend after her mother passed away in 2016 and revised to be less personal during the creation of this book around 2022–early 2023. So this is for my forever friend Sejavia Z. Campbell and for her little sister Jhania (I hope I spelled that right), young women still making their mom proud. I love you Javi, always, despite communication or distance. This is also for her best and longest friends, who have stuck by her before then and even more so now, Shanique A. Fletcher and Venecia.

'Vows' is written as an ode to my parents' marriage.

'Kiellettyjä Kirjoja' is written as a form of awareness or argument for Banned Book Week in September 2021. The meaning of the title is simply Banned Books, translated from English to Finnish based on their rankings in education globally. I was assisted with this poem by my very multi-talented friend Jaynelle Burchelle, and so it is dedicated to her. Thank you, hun.

'Questions of a Child: Answers to which I Never Learned' and 'Title: For the occupants of unmarked graves whose names I do not know and whose identities somehow resemble mine, we have forgotten to remember your swallowed body in the belly of Gaia; simply put, we have forgotten to remember you' was written in recognition of Black History Month.

'Imagine Depression is Funny Like That' is written to raise mental illness awareness. 'To be happy,' to bring awareness to suicide prevention, and my brother's attempt.

'Moon Flowers' represents the struggle Black women have faced throughout history and the sacrifices they have made to ensure they could live better. It also encapsulates that the history of abortion and Black women has not changed, regardless of the time period, and that contemporary women faced with challenges still sacrifice a lot.

'*Purple Letters*' was named by my then 4-year-old niece, as she decided to give me a color and a word to use to make a poem, and that's what I got, so that poem is for her, A'Zaria Smikle. Consequently, A'zaria can be credited with aiding in the creation of at least several other titles and being the sole inspiration for others.

'*Born to Die*' was named by an associate of mine, Denvor Greene (pen name, Dover Bleu). I wrote the poem but didn't know what to call it like all my other poems, and he came up with a name after reading it, so that one is dedicated to him.

'*The story of the drug dealer's daughter and love*' and '*XV things they never tell you about the offender's first victim*' were inspired by Sierra Freeman's 'Ten things you didn't know about the drug dealer's daughter'.

'*To my childhood friend B.A.D.*' for Bianca Dempster, my longest friend and one of the very first people to see my poetry and drawings. I love you. Thank you for being a part of my safe haven, despite not knowing it. Thank you for always encouraging me in art and poetry.

'*A lot like you*' inspired by Rudy Franscico

'*In memo-rum of the peers who never choose to stay past 22*' for Tory and Kurt, and 'The death of that girl; the rebirth of this woman' inspired by Alyssa Nicole Harris. 'Just another S.A. poem' inspired by Ebony Stewart

'*Permission to laugh*' inspired by Rachel Wiley's 'fat joke'.

'*I won't say don't date poets*' inspired by Whitney Hanson's 'I poetry we say'.

*** '*The story is told of a serial killer...*' was originally entitled '*The death of that girl; the rebirth of this woman*' and was the second of a two-part piece inspired by Alyssa Nicole Harris.

MEET THE ATHOR

Anne O'Kayé is a dedicated individual who, throughout a decade, has maintained a love and yearning to better understand various subjects, including criminology, history, and the arts. She is a voracious reader and spoken word aficionado; among her favorite authors are: James Patterson, Edwidge Danticat, Rick Riordan, J.K. Rowling, Steven King, Danielle Steel, and Robert Thier. Her favourite poets span from various structures and free forms. Her initial love of the craft started with the members of the rhetoric poetry group Passion for Christ ministries, more specifically the piece 'Ready or Not' performed by Janet Ikz and Ezekiel Azonwu.

Her penchant for the craft is stoked by her enthusiasm for

creativity and has been a place of peace, a safe haven, and one of many driving forces for her. While she acknowledges that she hasn't yet achieved what she aspires to, she remains grateful for the opportunities she has had and the potential she has discovered within herself.

Anne's guiding maxim, influenced by the quote from W.E.B. Du Bois, is that "There is no force greater than or equal to a woman who is determined to rise." She has maintained that such a woman is formidable, resilient, ambitious, and with God by her side, she is without a doubt destined for great things. Anne also emphasizes that women are only as strong as those around them, as potent as their prayers, and as devoted as they are allowed to be. In addition to her various interests, she enjoys drawing and performing her own unique poems on YouTube.

BEHIND THE BOOK COVER

The cover image of 'The Skeletons Within' is illustrated as red waves whose center a bound hand emerges, reaching out for a microphone. Though the author allows readers to have their own views of the cover and the feeling it evokes within them, she has nonetheless penned the actual thought process behind the image for readers who want to know exactly what it is about.

Ergo, The Red Sea, representing the blood shed of the first bombing in history (the bombing of Gronzy), serves as a sinkhole from which a mangled and desecrated hand bound in distress claws its way upwards towards salvation, barely holding onto a microphone, representing an ever-evading hope. Hope that is still healthy nonetheless, proving that even in the darkest of moments there is a silver lining, a sun preserving the greatness in you and willing it to grow. I hope that shows that the voice is not lost if you can still hold onto something.

The microphone speaks to poetry being a survival mechanism, a spoke in the wheel of an ever-evolving society. It speaks to warriors of the microphone: if a drowning man clutches at straws, how much more will an artist or creative clutch at a microphone to preserve their own soul from injustice and reflect the burdens and anger this world projects onto them? It speaks to breaching the chaos around. It gives light to a different day. The colors themselves are reflective of the promise of God to never destroy mankind by flooding the earth again yet synonymous with a creative making the promise to never be silenced again or dry drown from panic, even if it means emerging from the bombs they themselves have set.

The fingers are not fat; they are skinny and strangled, mimicking the illusion that they are bones and secrets uprooted and flourishing from pages of the past that continually flutter in the madness of the wings of hummingbirds. The cover design itself ties all this in to speak of poetry being the balm that satiates, the two-edged sword that both enables and robs; it speaks to the fulfillment of duty and of destiny where the most destroyed may find refuge and a community. It alludes to both history and gospel salvation and perseverance; it alludes to every theme; it alludes to every aspect of what you will encounter beyond the pages.

www.ingramcontent.com/pod-product-compliance
Lightning Source LLC
Chambersburg PA
CBHW030907120626
46554CB00001B/38